Tougher Than Leather

Tougher Than Leather

Bill Adler

Consafos Press

Consafos Press
PO Box 931568
Los Angeles, CA 90093

ISBN: 0-9656535-6-0

First published by New American Library in 1987
First Consafos Press trade paperback edition published 2002

Printed by American Book in Hong Kong

Contents

Foreword to the 2002 Edition

When this book was originally published in the spring of 1987, Run-DMC had been on a winning streak for the entirety of their four years in the music business. More to the point, most of us who worked with Run-DMC, as well as the crew themselves, figured that streak would never end. Even this book was supposed to be a sure thing, one-third of a genius cross-promotional trifecta. Suddenly there was going to be a new album by Run-DMC, a movie starring Run-DMC, and a book-length biography of Run-DMC, all of them entitled "Tougher Than Leather" and all of them exploding in the marketplace at the same pregnant moment.

Well, shit happens, and perhaps nowhere more frequently or distressingly than in the wonderful world of hip-hop. Both the album and the movie eventually joined the book in the light of day, but not at the same time. The album trailed the book by a full year and the movie skulked into theaters five months after the album—by which time our hopes of "cross-promotional synergy" had long since gone up in smoke. I could tell you why, but it's not an especially unusual story, nor a very instructive one. There were three separate teams working on three separate projects and there was virtually no coordination, even if our projects did share a name. The book was mostly ignored, the album found nowhere near as much favor as its predecessors, and the movie was panned even by hardcore hiphoppers.

And that was the end of Run-DMC's winning streak. They've continued to record and tour and produce, but they were never again as hot as they had been. This is no problem—at least with regard to history. Of course, Run-DMC *personally* would have preferred to reach even greater heights. But the fact remains that it is on the basis of the achievements recounted in this book that Run-DMC should be first-ballot shoo-ins for the Rock & Roll Hall of Fame when they become eligible in 2008. By the end of 1986 the aptly-dubbed Kings from Queens had long since conquered—and then vastly expanded—the kingdom of hiphop. They were the first rappers to earn a gold album (for 1984's *Run-DMC*), the first to earn a platinum album (for 1985's *King of Rock*), the first to earn a multi-platinum album (for 1986's *Raising Hell*), the first to see their videos played on MTV, the first to grace the cover of *Rolling Stone*, the first to perform on "American Bandstand"—and the *only* rap act to perform at LiveAid. By the end of '86 they had spearheaded three groundbreaking national rap tours and broken miles and miles of additional new ground in the spaces where rap would meet rock—an absolutely crucial contribution to hiphop's almost incidental racial reintegration of American pop. By the end of the decade, Run-DMC's dedication to b-boy style had earned them a salute from *Details* magazine as one of the handful of Most Important Fashion Influences of the Eighties.

Indeed, their impact has been nothing less than revolutionary. Although they debuted three-and-a-half years after Sugarhill Records and the Sugarhill Gang launched rap as a serious musical force, Run-DMC were the first to market tangible b-boy-ism, meaning the first to embody, without apology, the music, poetry, fashion, body language, and *worldview* of New York's black male teens—the hiphop culture that had been brewing underground for ten years when "It's Like That/Sucker MC's" dropped like a bomb in the spring of 1983.

But it's been fifteen years since this book was first issued, fifteen years in the lives of Run-DMC, fifteen years' worth of events, personal and professional, that are not described here—as well as fifteen years during which hiphop culture has grown well beyond everyone's wildest dreams. Some of the crew's personal trials in this latter period were covered—or rather uncovered—in a "Behind the Music" special produced by VH-1 in 2000: Run's suicidal tendencies in the wake of the group's decline and the reclamation of his faith and purpose as the born-again Reverend Run, DMC's successful battle against alcoholism and his first exploratory efforts to launch a solo career, Jay's unfortunate tendency as a younger man to get caught up in violence. There've been marriages and divorces, children born, and creative ventures entered into individually that have nothing to do with Run-DMC as a group. In the past two years, Run, DMC, and Russell Simmons (Run's older brother and the group's manager) have all written books about their lives and careers—and surely there will be more to come.

Still, this little book captures a moment—the rise of Run-DMC before the fall. There are portraits of Hollis, Queens, of Run-DMC's parents, and of the guys themselves as youths. There's a lot about the early life and career of Russell Simmons. There's a visit to Disco Fever, the most important nightclub in hiphop history. There's an account of the launch of Def Jam Recordings, arguably hiphop's most successful and enduring label, and a portrait of Rick Rubin, the hugely talented producer who co-founded the label with Russell. We're with Run-DMC on tour in America, England, and Japan, on stage at LiveAid, on the set of "Krush Groove," and on the campuses of Columbia and Princeton, where they join the international fight against South African apartheid in the years before Nelson Mandela's release from jail. We're also with them in the studio during the making of the three albums that will win them their place in history.

Reading the book anew, I was pleased to discover that I had been reasonably successful in capturing the sound and flavor of Run, D, and Jay's voices in conversation—their rhythm, passion, individuality, optimism, and good humor. I also noticed that I paid a lot of attention to how the exploits of the crew were covered in the mass media, which was perhaps only natural given my background as a journalist and my job as Run-DMC's publicist. I'm hopeful that that story—the story of the myriad weird ways in which these alien young hiphoppers were reflected in media which had never before grappled with hiphop—will also resonate with contemporary readers.

Of course, even as Run-DMC recedes as hitmakers, the hiphop culture they embodied so successfully roars on. Los Angeles was producing great rap by the late Eighties. A few years later, important talent began to erupt out of Miami, Oakland, Houston, and Seattle. During the last ten years platinum rappers have emerged from New Orleans, Atlanta, Memphis, St. Louis, Detroit and North Carolina. Will Smith is a bigger movie star than Sidney Poitier ever was. Lyor Cohen, who started in the rap music business as Run-DMC's road manager, is now president and CEO of the Island/Def Jam Music Group, a huge division of the largest record company in the world, overseeing a pop domain of which rap is only a part. Russell Simmons has evolved into a king of all hiphop media—music, television, movies, fashion, magazine publishing, advertising, the internet—and has recently begun to invest considerable energy into national electoral politics. Although we have not yet seen a presidential candidate who takes "Together Forever" as his campaign theme song, it may be just a matter of time.

You could say that it all started here. Enjoy.

Bill Adler
New York City
April 16, 2002

Acknowledgments

There's no way I would have been able to research and write this book as quickly as was necessary without the generous help of my friends, colleagues, and family.

I'd therefore like to thank my friend Gary Harris for introducing me to Allan Sonnenschein at Penthouse, who confirmed my long-held conviction that there was a book in the career of Run-DMC, and who introduced me to his agent Barbara Lowenstein. I'd also like to thank Barbara for tackling the project, and her associate Lori Perkins, for taking it to Gary Luke at New American Library, who became my editor. And thanks to Kenneth B. Anderson, Esq., for nailing down the legal details.

My friends and co-workers at Rush Productions and Def Jam Recordings in New York were just great, as usual, and combined to cover for me while I took a leave of absence from the day-to-day whirlwind that is Rush. In particular, I'd like to thank Russell Simmons, Heidi Smith, Bill Stephney, Lyor

Cohen, Lisa Cortes, Simone Reyes, Dante Ross, and Hank Shocklee, a clutch pinch hitter if ever there was one.

My friends in the music business were likewise very helpful. They include Larry Smith, Trevor Gale, Cory Robbins and Chris LaSalle at Profile Records, Ricky Walker of Cedric Walker & Associates, Darryll Brooks and Carol Kirkendall of G Street Express, Jeff Sharp of Stageright Productions, Steve Loeb and Ruddy Hui of Greene Street Recording, Steve Gett and Eloise Bryan of Chung King, House of Metal, Nick Gold at Entertainment Travel, Betty Hisiger at "Friday Night Videos," and Lori Somes at the Howard Bloom Organization, who was especially helpful.

The following writers conducted interviews with Run-DMC from which I plucked telling quotes: John Leland for *Spin*, Steve Dougherty for *People*, Nelson George for the *Village Voice*, Robert Hilburn for the *Los Angeles Times*, Alan Sonnenschein for *Penthouse*, Toby Goldstein for *Creem*, Richard Grabel for *New York Talk*, John Anderson for the *Daily Texan*, Barry Walters for the *Village Voice*, Scott Mehno for the *East Village Eye*, and Sue Cummings for *Spin*. Special thanks to Greg Tate at the *Village Voice*, Jim Canosa at *Billboard*, and Eugene Brown, formerly of the *Queens College Phoenix*.

Thanks to Ed Kerby, Roger Aldi and Greg Mack at KDAY, Los Angeles, for providing me with airchecks of the "Day of Peace" broadcast. Thanks to Leon Watkins of L.A.'s Community Youth Gang Services for background information on the gang situation in southern California.

Thanks to Dave Sims, for providing me with all sorts of information about (and flyers from!) the early days of Rush Productions.

Thanks to my dear aunt, Vivian Adler, and to Eric Weisbard, both of Princeton, New Jersey.

Many thanks, of course, to the families of Run-DMC: Daniel Simmons (senior and junior), Shirley Simmons, Evelyn Simmons, Byford and Bannah McDaniels, and Connie Mizell.

Thanks to my father and mother, Marvin and Esther Adler, for a timely loan and the lifetime of love and encouragement that preceded it.

I thank heaven for my wife, Sara Moulton, who kept me sane throughout the time I was writing the book. Our marriage is a blessing.

Finally, many thanks to Run-DMC—Joseph Simmons, Darryl McDaniels, and Jason Mizell—for opening up their early lives to me, for making such tremendous music, and for having the courage to set an example for their fans. It is an honor to know and to work with them.

Bill Adler
New York City
April 6, 1987

Tougher Than Leather

A NIGHT OF WAR, A DAY OF PEACE

It was about nine o'clock on Sunday, August 17, 1986, when Run, DMC, and Jam Master Jay, the three members of Run-DMC, pulled up in a limo backstage at the Long Beach Arena, 35 minutes south of Los Angeles. It was supposed to be just another night's work, the 56th date on the 64-date American leg of the Raising Hell Tour, which starred Run-DMC and their fellow rappers and New York City homeboys, Whodini, LL Cool J, and the Beastie Boys.

Of course, being part of the greatest rap act in the world and having yet another chance to stand up onstage in front of 14,000 fans, shouting out your own rhymes and getting paid big money to do so, is nice work if you can get it—and DMC, for one, was looking forward to getting busy.

"I had my forty-dogs on ice, a new suit, and a haircut," he recalls. "I was ready to have *fun!*"

3

As it turned out, fun was in short supply that night, and Run-DMC never even got a chance to hit the stage. By the time they arrived, the Long Beach Arena had been for over an hour and a half in the grip of perhaps the worst rock'n'roll riot in history. Hundreds of marauding gangsters from competing youth gangs had chosen the arena as the latest battleground in their ongoing war, and now they were not only at each other's throats, they were terrorizing the thousands of young fans who were there for the music, and the music only.

It is not widely known outside of Los Angeles, but L.A. is gang heaven. Some 400 gangs boast over 50,000 members. They've been a hard fact of life in the city for years, but the recent emergence of crack—an extremely potent and inexpensive form of smokable cocaine—has turned a bad problem into what singing star and L.A. native Barry White has been calling "the coming Armageddon at your front door."

Of course, the tour had been prepared for *some* trouble. Most of rap music's millions of fans are teenagers, and there's always the possibility of unruliness when thousands of teenagers get together. With that in mind, the concert's promoters had made the ticket holders in Long Beach (like kids wherever the tour played) pass through metal detectors and submit to a physical pat-down before they were allowed to go to their seats. Inside the arena, there were 85 unarmed private security guards, 42 armed security guards (stationed in the lobby), and 50 female ushers. Outside there were half-a-dozen Long Beach police officers on motorcycles handling traffic, and another nine stationed around the building.

Normally it would have been enough. Although there'd been problems in a handful of cities outside the arena, after the show, and the odd scuffle or two inside the hall, there'd never been a full-scale riot inside the arena during any of the Raising Hell Tour's shows. But this time, the security people later agreed, nothing short of an army could have prevented the disruption. As Detective Steve Young told *Rolling Stone*: "There are long-held grudges between these gangs, and when they converge in one place, the paybacks will come."

Run and D and J could see it all from backstage. The building manager had thrown on the houselights, a move that generally embarrasses unruly citizens into civilized behavior, but the ploy wasn't working this night. There was Jalil Hutchins of Whodini, up onstage pleading with the fighting kids to cool it—and getting nowhere. The gangsters had torn the legs off the arena's folding metal chairs and were now using them to club their enemies. Shots were being fired at the front and at the back of the arena, kids were being thrown from the balcony, and the gangs were on the move. The private security crews, mostly made up of retired reserved and off-duty police officers, were running in in crews of six and eight —and getting run right out again by posses of 60 and 80.

"You could see them walking through the crowd like a herd of elephants stomping on a crowd of ants," recalled Jam Master Jay. "It was like a stampede—chairs coming up in the air, panicked kids in the crowd, knowing the gangs were coming their way and couldn't get out," said Run. "You could see 300 people all moving against one section, beating and robbing them. I was really scared for our fans out there."

Ten minutes later, the crew had reason to be scared for

themselves. Security had finally convinced them to move into their dressing room, where they were joined by Vanessa Williams, the former Miss America, and LeVar Burton, who'd played Kunte Kinte in "Roots." Nobody could see what was going on, but they could *hear* as well as they needed to. D remembers a message coming over a walkie-talkie—"We're losing it! We're losing it!"—and then one of the security guards coming to their room.

"Yo, don't lock the door," he said.

"Why not?"

"'Cause when they come back here, I'm comin' in with y'all!"

That's when Run-DMC tore up one of the dressing room's clothes racks to fashion weapons for themselves. "If they come in here, we gonna *definitely* chase them back out," said D. "I want to be the big motherfuckin' Bruce Lee and kick the gang's ass, throw them all in fuckin' jail and do my concert," Jay said. In fact, Run-DMC never had to engage the gangs in hand-to-hand combat. Gangsters *did* try to crash the backstage area, but they were turned back at the small entranceway, where security guards had hastily thrown up a barricade.

Finally the police arrived. At 11:02, three-and-a-half hours after the promoters had begun calling for help, sixty baton-wielding cops in riot gear entered the rear of the arena. They spent the next fifteen minutes clearing out the place while a helicopter overhead ordered people to disperse. The final tally was five stabbed, one shot, four arrests, and 41 treated for injuries at local hospitals.

The next day at a press conference Run said, "Those kids have nothing to do with Run-DMC. They're scumbags and roaches, and they would have hit me in the head, too," adding that he thought that the gangs were "running" L.A., and swearing not to return "until the local authorities get the problem under control." The crew then cancelled the show set for that night at the Hollywood Palladium.

That same day radio station KDAY received what the *Los Angeles Weekly* described as "a tidal wave of calls from sympathetic fans wanting to let the rappers know that they were sorry for what happened"—and begging the crew not to punish all of Los Angeles for the misdeeds of a few. Three days after the riot the arena's manager announced that he would no longer book shows "with a history of violence."

Suddenly, however, it looked as if the crew's luck was about to change. On August 22nd, five days after the riot, the mayor's office invited Run-DMC to assemble, and then to headline, an anti-gang, anti-drug concert on the steps of City Hall at the annual Los Angeles Street Scene Festival on September 20. Unfortunately, the city then proceeded to *disinvite* them on September 15 and to blame the group for the violence at Long Beach. Deputy Mayor Tom Huston insisted, "I'll be damned if we'll have them," piously claiming that the Street Scene Festival was "a family-oriented event" whose patrons he had no intention of subjecting to "any possible threat of gang violence."

So Run-DMC stayed home—and there was trouble anyway, a debacle described by the *Los Angeles Times* as "a mini-riot staged by angry drunk punk rockers," which resulted in 25 arrests and one death. Just as Jam Master Jay had claimed, it appeared that "Run-DMC is not the problem; L.A. is the problem."

Three weeks later the crew were back in Los Angeles at the

invitation of radio station KDAY, which had cooked up something called A Day of Peace, aimed at inspiring a peace treaty between warring gangs, and inaugurating a whole season of peace that would last past the upcoming Thanksgiving and Christmas holidays and into the new year. The explosive combination of gang warfare and drugs had that year been taking a heavy toll among KDAY's listeners, primarily the black youth of Los Angeles: 136 murders through October 9, the Day of Peace itself, including twelve during the weekend just prior to the broadcast.

The idea was the kids of the community would be able to call KDAY, talk directly about their troubled lives to Run-DMC, and maybe find some direction and inspiration there. Run-DMC had been KDAY's number-one group ever since music director Greg Mack had installed the station's rap-heavy format—60-70% of the records aired were by rappers—in September of 1983. The media and the city may've been blaming the gang problem on Run-DMC, but the kids and KDAY knew better.

So did Leon Watkins, the 41-year-old regional director of the Community Youth Gang Services. "At this point Run-DMC are the best anti-drug and anti-gang spokesmen in the country. No one commands more respect than they do," he said. "Kids listen to them, and when a kid sits down and listens, he thinks."

Run himself was equally optimistic. "We feel we're in charge of all the kids," he said at the press conference the day before the broadcast. "Kids listen to us before they listen to their parents or teachers, even, because we're cooler and we're positive."

The powers-that-be were skeptical. "If these kids aren't

going to listen to authorities, I doubt they're going to listen to a rap group," huffed Officer Roger Magnuson of the LAPD's Community Resources Against Street Hoodlums (a/k/a CRASH). "I think that they are taking a very simple solution to a very complex problem."

A frankly hostile *Rolling Stone* account of the event noted that "outside the studio dozens of husky security guards expected trouble" on the Day of Peace itself, and quoted "a nervous worker at the event" saying that "this whole thing is a farce. Kids with Uzi's and sawed-off shotguns are not going to stop their shit because of a radio program."

Inside, KDAY News Director Roger Aldi opened up the mike at four o'clock and announced the station's telephone number. With him and Run-DMC in the studio were Barry White, Olympic boxing champ Paul Gonzales, and Leon Watkins. Gonzales had grown up in gangs in the *barrios* of East Los Angeles before turning to boxing. White's brother had been killed by gang violence only a couple of years earlier, and White himself claimed to have been a member of a gang in south Los Angeles before turning to the recording career that won him international stardom in the early Seventies.

Now Aldi turned to Run and said, "What's the message?"

"I'd like to tell the kids who are thinking about joining gangs and doing drugs not to do it," replied Run. "It's not right. You *know* it's not right. I don't like it, and my mama don't like it neither."

Aldi, playing the devil's advocate, said, "Forgive me, but we've heard this before. Why should this make a difference now?"

Jam Master Jay had the answer. "Because they never heard it from *us* before. *You* always tell 'em. Somebody *old* always tell 'em. Now they're hearing it from me. I'm young now. I was just in high school a little while ago." In fact, both Jay and Run were 21. DMC was 22. "And I *am* the street," Jay continued. "So if something bad's happening on the street, something bad's happening to me. I know it ain't right, and I'm telling them it ain't right. *That's* why it's different."

And it was different. During the next two hours between ten thousand and fifteen thousand callers attempted to make contact with Run-DMC, an overload so severe that it burned out phone circuits throughout the Crenshaw area.

Even more telling than the number of calls were the types of questions directed to the rappers, questions that indicated that Run-DMC's fans thought of them as far more than just another pop group, serious questions like "Why do young people take drugs?" and "Why do innocent people get killed?" and "How long do you think that this is going to go on?"

And then there was the testifying, the recitation of horror stories capable of making one's hair stand on end: the young boy who saw his drug-abusing older brother grab his infant sister out of his mother's hands and throw the child on the floor, killing her; the high school girl from "the Valley" (the "nice" part of L.A.), whose best friend was shot to death while waiting for a bus, "and a month ago my friend Ronny got killed, too;" the ten-year-old girl whose mother had put her on the street to sell drugs; the high school boy who sold drugs so that he'd have the money to buy the clothes he needed to "look fresh," and who asked in sincere puzzlement, "At 16 what else am I supposed to be thinking about?"

It was hard to argue with the twisted logic behind some of the calls. With unemployment among black youth standing at 40 percent and the quality of education so low that there are 19-year-olds in L.A. who not only can't read or write, they can't even tell time, it's little wonder that—as Steve Valdivia, executive director of CYGS, points out—"Drugs have become part of the economy in south Los Angeles." Or, as a caller named Marie put it, "Selling drugs gives people a hundred dollars a day or more, and to work at McDonald's, where they're only hiring kids to make $3.50 an hour, is kind of stupid."

Then there was "Elton," who "grew up in the gangs," and said, "When I was thirteen I was straight gangbanging. Fourteen and fifteen I was selling drugs. Sixteen and seventeen I was pimping. That kind of life is you live fast, you die fast. That life led me nowhere. At 21 years old they left me for dead. They had shot me in the head three times. I had multiple stab wounds, multiple gunshot wounds, multiple lacerations, and the doctors said they didn't understand why I was alive."

The day's panelists had stories of their own. "Like people claim about being from Vietnam, well, I'm from the streets of East L.A.," said Paul Gonzales. "I'm a veteran of gang warfare. I got involved with gangs when I was seven years old. I ran with them for a lot of years. I got shot when I was 12 years old, got stabbed when I was 13."

Run, referring to Hollis, Queens, where he and D and Jay all grew up and still lived, said, "The name of the game is Beat the Street where we live, too. And it's a hard thing to do, but you can do it if you just find out what you like to do best, and then go for it from there."

Jam Master Jay, who'd run in his early teens with a little "posse" of his own called the Hollis Crew, said, "Whoever's in a gang is scared—'I'm selling drugs, I gotta watch my back.

I'm scared of the cops. I'm scared this guy is gonna stick me up. I'm scared that I'm gonna die.' And all the gang members, in themselves, know they're wrong. They *know* they don't want their little brother wid it 'cause they don't want their little brother scared like they are."

DMC, the group's Quiet Storm, suggested forming "good gangs" to play ball with and to go to school with—which is pretty much what the members of Run-DMC had done when *they* were kids.

Finally, the show ran out of time. Leon Watkins gave out the telephone numbers to the CYGS 24-hour hotlines, and then the members of Run-DMC broke into one of their most famous raps: "Now the things I do make me a star/And you can be too if you know who you are/Just put your mind to it, you'll go real far/Like the pedal to the metal when you're driving a car."

It turned out that bass-voiced Barry White, no mean rapper himself, also had a rhyme for the occasion, and he weighed in with it as soon as Run-DMC had finished with theirs: "Life will always be a test/If you wanna win, you gotta give it your best. . . . "

As quickly as Barry had begun, Jam Master Jay began softly singing the groovy little ascending/descending rhythmic hook that went with one of Barry's biggest hits, a song called "I'm Gonna Love You Just a Little More, Babe."

"Ba do-do-do-dooooom," sang Jay. "Doo doo doo da-doom. . . . "

"Life will always be unkind . . . " rapped Barry.

"Ba do-do-do-da-doooooom. . . . "

" . . . to those who just keep wasting time . . . "

"Do do do da-doom. . . . "

Everyone laughed. And then Roger reminded the crew that "this is just a beginning. We can't solve the world's problems in two hours. But we do hope this is the first day of a very long-lasting peace."

In fact, no big surprise, Run-DMC and their friends did not solve ten year's worth of gang problems in Los Angeles in two hours. But what they did accomplish was pretty remarkable anyway. It turned out that young gangsters all over the city had been listening. The CYGS hotline reported that it had received over 500 calls during the broadcast from gang members wanting to know how to get out, for information about drugs. Even more remarkable, Leon Watkins claims that the broadcast directly inspired members of the Crips and the Bloods, two of the largest and most notorious of L.A.'s gangs, to sign a peace treaty a few weeks later.

But the most astonishing result of the Day of Peace was that it had fulfilled the modest goal explicit in its name. That night KCBS-TV news announced that there hadn't been a single incident of gang-related violence reported that day. During a season that was seeing from ten to fifteen gang-related incidents *every day* —including murder, burglary, robbery, assault, car theft, and drive-by shootings—in a year that would go down on record as the most violent in the history of the city of Los Angeles, KDAY's Day of Peace, built around a rap group named Run-DMC, was entirely peaceful.

Leon Watkins, even given his early optimism, was stunned. "This has *never* happened before," he said.

Run himself couldn't have been prouder. At the end of the year he told *People* magazine: "I'm so big in L.A. that when I talked—like E.F. Hutton—they listened."

ONE

Back In the Day

There's no way to understand Run-DMC and the kind of music they make—and why kids listen when they speak—without understanding Hollis, the suburban neighborhood in the borough of Queens in the city of New York where all three members of the crew grew up and where they all continue to live.

Hollis was seventy percent white when Daniel Simmons moved there with his pregnant wife Evelyn and their two oldest sons—Daniel Jr., 11, and Russell, 7—on November 1, 1964, just 14 days before Joseph—who would one day be known as Run—was born.

Daniel Sr.'s written remembrance paints Hollis as "a place made for people who dream of a green lawn, a patio, and genial people next door who smiled and seemed to be welcoming us." He further recalls city services and local amenities in abundance. "The Parks Department trimmed the trees without our even asking. Sanitation men came like clockwork. The buses rolled regularly to and from the subway. The neighborhood had two meat markets, two drug stores, a florist, an A&P, and a Dan's Supermarket. Local merchants came by on Saturday mornings to deliver eggs, butter, and freshly baked bread. The local schools, PS134 and IS192, were exceptional." In sum, he wrote, "We were an integrated neighborhood with all the rights white people are heir to."

Suddenly, however, things began to change. The Simmonses woke up one morning to discover that their white next-door neighbors had moved in the night, and then "like smoke" were gone. "It was as if we were the Black Plague," Daniel Sr. continued. "Real estate agents did a brisk business, and by the time Joseph was ten the neighborhood was all black." City services and local amenities began to disappear. "Up the side streets people still cut lawns and painted their houses," he concluded. "They still cared about their children and did not despair when the bakers closed and the meat merchants fled. They did not give up when Hollis Avenue became drug-infested and took their children on the march of death. Hollis was alive and in some instances well. But distrust and despair is part of our make-up. And why not?"

The Hollis in which the members of Run-DMC grew up, then, was not at all a slum, but it was a ghetto, a ghetto in the suburbs. And every kid who grew up there, according to Run's older brother Russell, had a choice: "We could either stay on the block, which was nice, or we could go to the corner, which was like *the corner* in any other neighborhood in the city. On the corner two blocks from us was a big heroin house. Now it's a crack corner."

The Block or the Corner. The Bellerose on 239th Street and Hollis Avenue—where you could see the big Hollywood smashes of the day—or the Loew's (pronounced LOW-eez) on Jamaica Avenue, which ran a kind of informal repertory series of the great blaxploitation flicks of the Seventies, movies like "Super Fly," "The Mack," "Uptown Saturday Night," "Truck Turner," and "Shaft in Africa." Hollis was 15 minutes by car along the expressway to the heart of the slums of the Bronx, and five minutes by car to Jamaica Estates, the wealthy neighborhood where New York's Mayor Koch owns a house.

The Block or the Corner. All three members of Run-DMC had friends in both places, and it was that ability to move from one pole to the other—and to avoid getting pulled permanently into life on the Corner—that has made them tougher than leather.

More than anything or anyone else, it was Run-DMC's parents who taught them what they needed to know to navigate safely and intelligently in Hollis. "It helped us so much to have parents who are as wise as ours," says Run. "I knew by the time I was ten what was good and what was bad, and I always tried to be on the good side. Other kids grow up bad because that's all they're taught. And you don't get a chance to learn if nobody teaches you."

Highly educated themselves, Run's folks, to begin with, are naturally inclined to teach. Daniel and Evelyn Simmons met as students at Howard University, where he got his BA in history and his MA in English, and she received degrees in sociology and psychology. Eventually both landed respectable long-term jobs; he as the attendance supervisor for Queens School District 29 and she as a recreation director for the New York City Department of Parks.

In July 1963 Daniel Simmons Sr. was a comfortable, home-owning member of the black middle-class when he went through the experience that, he says, "changed my whole life."

"I had been trying to be more white than black," he recalls. "I knew more about Friedrich Nietzsche than I did about Frederick Douglass." He also knew that he was vainly "looking for a way to be a part of that great movement," the national civil rights movement led by Dr. Martin Luther King.

"One day," he says, "right around the corner from where I lived, there They were." *They* were the builders of the development of Rochdale Village in Queens, and they were doing so with an all-white crew, which violated federal labor laws. The building project was already being demonstrated against by members of the NAACP and CORE, and Mr. Simmons joined the line. "I felt compelled," he recalls. "I felt that if I didn't do this I would never be able to live with myself."

A few weeks later, having become one of the leaders of the demonstration, he sat himself down in front of an oncoming cement truck and declared, "I will not be moved." He wasn't either, until the police picked him up off the ground and arrested him. Mr. Simmons says going to jail was "like a religious experience," and thinks of that summer on the picket line as "coming from the Valley of Indifference to the Plain of Significance."

He turned 40 on the picket line, and a few weeks later was on a bus with the rest of the Jamaica chapter of the NAACP heading for the August 28th "Freedom March" in Washington, D.C., where they would join the two hundred thousand others present to hear Dr. King himself deliver the immortal "I have a dream" speech.

A story that later appeared in the *Queens College Phoenix*

catches Daniel Sr. in action that day. "The captain of one of the city buses was Danny Simmons, a Dick Gregory on wheels. . . . He brightened the atmosphere by suggesting that the bus be named the Constitution because it was moving so slowly. And he expressed the fear that some people thought that NAACP stood for 'Never Aggravated Adam Clayton Powell.'"

Looking back recently, Mr. Simmons said, "I think I passed on that kind of controlled anger at social injustice to all my sons."

For all of his learning and experience, however, and for all of his fears as a parent about the trouble his kids could fall into, Mr. Simmons is not a snob about life on the Corner. "You'd better not be walking around here and be so hincty you can't speak to dudes on the corner," he says. "The more of them you know, the better off you are if you ever get in trouble: 'There's my man!' They come right in for you."

"That's the way I lived my life," he continues. "All the kids I knew when I was coming up in the ghetto in Baltimore went to jail. I was playing football one day and the cops came and took the whole line to jail! I was standing back there, waiting for the ball to be snapped, and I said, 'Damn, I got nobody to block!' These guys had been robbing drugstores, every drugstore but the one I worked in. We were 16 years old."

Both of the Simmonses' oldest sons went to the Corner. By the time Daniel Jr. was fifteen, he was a self-described "hippie gangster" known around the way as T.O.D., short for Tripped-Out Danny. A brilliant student, he was also the Minister of Revolutionary Culture of his high school's Black Student Union—which meant that when he and his crew took over the principal's office, it was up to Danny to play Jimi Hendrix—interspersed with selected readings from the works of Malcolm X and Chairman Mao—over the public address system. He was finally suspended for coming to school with a suitcase full of Molotov cocktails, a concoction he'd learned to prepare by reading Abbie Hoffman's "Steal This Book"—which Danny had.

More a hippie than a revolutionary, Danny attended Lincoln University in Pennsylvania, "the black Antioch," for two years (living the whole time in the girls' dorm), left there "under a cloud," and finally graduated from New York University with a major in sociology and a minor in philosophy. He went on to earn a master's degree in public administration from Long Island University. Today he sells real estate in Brooklyn to buy himself the time he needs to do what he really wants—paint and write. His most recent novel is entitled, "I'm Moving to Wisconsin, Gonna Sell Heroin to the Christians."

The Simmonses' second son, Russell, was also drawn to the Corner. He was a good student at August Martin High School and an athlete talented enough to make the baseball team, but "baseball wasn't cool," he recalls. "I sold reefer the whole time I was in high school and I hung out, mostly."

In the tenth grade Russell was a member of the 17th Division of the Seven Immortals, a huge gang with chapters all over the city. The gang scene in New York then, in the early Seventies, was nearly as widespread (if not as violent) as the one in Los Angeles now. Gangs like the Seven Crowns, the Jolly Stompers, and the Black Spades had been around for *generations*. Toward the end of his gang adventure, Russ was made warlord of the Hollis chapter, which alone had about 800 members. Their colors, painted onto bluejean jackets with no sleeves, consisted of a lightning bolt shot through a big 7, with the word "Seven" around the top of the design and "Immortals" on the bottom.

"Our gang wasn't money-oriented that much," Russ recalls. "We used to break into parties and never pay for nothing, that kind of shit. We'd go out to see whatever was hot and cheap on Jamaica Avenue in Queens—shows with the Delfonics, the Dramatics, the Moments, the Temptations. And while these groups were singing their sweet love ballads, the worst gang fights you'd ever seen would break out."

Russell asserts there was nothing about the music itself that caused the violence. "There was always a fight because that's what happens when you get 800 kids under one roof, at night, drinking. It was no problem." And, alluding to the sensational media coverage of the violence that followed a few of the Raising Hell Tour's shows in the summer of 1986, he adds, "It wasn't newsworthy, that's for sure."

For his part, Russell went to the shows not just because he was in a gang and it was "something to do," but because he truly loved the music—particularly a certain beat in the music. He remembers as an eight-grader owning an eight-track cassette copy of an album by the Pointer Sisters with a song called "Yes We Can Can." "The first eight bars are what sold me that record," he says, and he sings the rolling, funky, New Orleans-styled rhythm by memory. "But I had to keep rewinding the whole damn tape just to hear those eight bars. 'Use Me' by Bill Withers was also that kind of record. Al Green always had a beat, too, and the Temptations, and the very first record by the Chi-Lites, *before* 'You Got to Give More Power to the People.'

"Those beats all had something in common to me, and I don't think they did to anybody else. And I really think that's what's special about all rap records, all hiphop records, and all the R&B records I produce," he continues, referring to records by artists from Run-DMC to Oran "Juice" Jones, Chuck Stanley, and Alyson Williams. "That rhythm is something I always gravitated toward, even before there was a name for it."

Russell left the Seven Immortals when he was 16, having decided that "what we did was boring and pointless." He did, however, stick with the reefer sales. His corner was Hollis Avenue near the park at 205th Street, just down the block from his parents' house. "Hollis and Two-Fifth was a hot spot, and that was *our spot.* I sold *so much* reefer up there."

It was hardly a Chamber of Commerce-approved enterprise, but Russell *was* demonstrating impressive amounts of initiative, independence, and stick-to-it-iveness. He worked most nights from seven o'clock or so until one in the morning and, on a good night, walked away with $400.

That's when the real fun began. "We'd go to whichever discos were open, drink champagne, and act like hustlers." Russell smiles broadly as he says this, but his tone is touched with disbelief at the magnitude of his own youthful achievements. "You know what I'm saying? You're seventeen years old, and you gotta be nineteen to get in, and you in? You gotta have shoes, and you all in sneakers, sitting up at the bar with a bottle of champagne? You the best motherfucker! You win, for sure."

Russ graduated from high school in the spring of 1975 and enrolled that fall as a sociology major at the Harlem campus of the City College of New York. He'd chosen sociology, he says, because "it was very easy. Anything that you're good at, you like, right? And it was easy to be good at sociology, so I had to like it." And, in the interests of accumulating some pocket money, he kept on selling that reefer

Russ was a pretty diligent student his first two years, but he also spent time hanging out and working with a group of party promoters, learning his first lessons in the music business. "My whole posse promoted shows," Russ remembers.

It was also during this period, around 1977, that Russell saw his first rapper in action. It was at the Charles Gallery, over by the Apollo Theater on 125th Street, just a little 250-seat club owned at the time by singer Melba Moore, less than fifteen blocks from the CCNY campus. "Eddie Cheba was on the mike and he just fucked me up," Russ says. "He was a student over at Bronx Community College, about my age, and he had a real popular radio show on WFUV, the college station. He was a funny-looking dude, used to wear a baseball cap all the time, and a little plaid sports-jacket. . . .

"Easy Gee was up in the deejay booth cutting that night, and they'd passed the mike cord down to Eddie in front." Ten years later Russell remembers nearly every detail of Cheba's routine. "'It's the Cheba, girl! It's Eddie Cheba Night! Now, look here, it's on Thursday, every Thursday, and we gonna do it like this . . .'"

Up in the deejay booth, Easy Gee took his cue and dropped the beat to Parliament's "Flashlight." Like Russell, Easy Gee was after the beat and the beat only. He had no use for the song's vocal. He'd just play its huffy, tuba-like bass line over and over again, cutting to his second turntable after the first had used up that bass line, and then re-cueing it while the second burned up the eight bars or so of worthwhile material.

Meanwhile, Eddie was revving up the crowd. "It's Cheba Cheba chee-chee-chee-Cheba/Up my back and around my neck, *Ooh ah!* Got the girl in check/Come on, come on, you do the Jerk/Let me see your body work/Slam dunk, feel the funk, come on come on, shake your rump. . . . "

Out on the floor, the dancers were definitely doing their part. Dave Sims, an early associate of Russ, remembers Eddie as "the number-one party motivator at that time. He really knew how to make the crowd participate. He would have his cheerleaders with him, three cute girls wearing t-shirts that read 'the Cheba Crew,' and they led the crowd with all the answers."

Eddie rapped, "On and on and on and on, we'll do this shit to the break of dawn/Said on and on and on and on/Like hot butter on what—?" And the crowd screamed, "Popcorn!" Eddie'd ask, "Who makes it sweeter?" And the crowd screamed, "Cheba Cheba Cheba!" He'd say, "Let's stop," and the crowd yelled, "Let's go!" He'd say, "Let's rock," and they screamed, "Let's roll!"—and every time the crowd did their bit, Easy Gee would cut off the music entirely, so that all you got was the deafening roar from the dancers, and then the music rushing back right on beat. Russ is still thrilled at the thought of it all. "It was so def, and people had so much fun," he says.

By the fall of 1977, when Russ was ready to go out on his own as a party promoter, he knew that the kind of party he wanted to promote would feature rappers. It was a daring concept. At the time, during the heyday of disco, every would-be slickster from Boston to Beirut was blow-drying his hair, strapping on his patent leather shoes, and striding down the streets to the beat of "Ah-ah-ah-ah, stayin' alive, stayin' alive."

But Russ had seen that now there were hundreds and maybe thousands of people who shared his passion for this new music. He knew he could throw a party and not play a Bee Gees record all night, and he'd still draw a crowd. It might be a rough crowd, but Russ's experience on the corner had brought him into contact with many a rough kid. And besides, disco was, in Russ's opinion, simply "too nervous," that is, too fast and funkless to dance to.

The posse Russ put together to help with his promotions included an aspiring rapper who called himself Kool DJ Kurt. They were an odd couple, Russell and Kurtis. Kurt was from a broken home in Harlem and had been on the streets "scrambling" from the time he was 14. He'd rapped a little, but he'd hung out a lot more. His birth name was Kurtis Walker. He'd recently graduated from New York's Music and Arts High School and enrolled as a communications major at CCNY, which was just down the block from where he'd grown up. "Kurt wasn't popular then. He wasn't even popular in Harlem," Russell remembers, "but he was my man."

Kurtis, for his part, has said, "At first I thought Russ was kind of soft, you know, like a Queens kid. He was trying to be street, like a lot of kids from nice homes. I used to see him around the clubs with the wild clothes and the Stetson hat. But Russell was smarter and more ambitious than most of the other guys around, and I liked him." Indeed, Russ and Kurt liked the same kind of music and shared the same sense of style in clothes and accessories. They were among the very first to wear gold nameplates around their necks, a fashion that didn't become a widespread fad until several years later.

Russ' high energy had already earned him the nickname Rush—which is what his nameplate spelled out—and he advertised his earliest productions with the slogan: "Rush—the Force in College Parties." Rush threw his very first show at a club called the Renaissance in Queens. He had rented the club for $500 and spent an additional $300 buying 20,000 flyers and a thousand stickers for street promotion.

The flyers and stickers were crucial. "The more flyers and stickers and posters you got your name on, the more popular you'd become as a rapper or a promoter," says Russ. It was Dave Sims's job to "ride the track" and distribute those stickers and flyers all over town. "We'd hit five or six clubs, handing out flyers, then we'd get on the trains and stick up posters all over Manhattan, the Bronx, Queens—ducking cops the whole time," Dave recalled. "You can only do that stuff in the middle of the night because it's against the law. So it was always a little adventure, running down Broadway at four in the morning, nobody but you and the cops out at that time of night."

About 800 people showed up at a place that held 600, Russell remembered of that first party. "A lot of Harlem came, a lot of City College, but also a lot of people from Queens. It was the best party, the greatest mixture of people you've ever seen, and they were all our friends. And that's how Rush Productions became important. Our parties were different."

Kool DJ Kurt, renamed Kurtis Blow by Russell, provided the rap that night. He was short, lean, and good-looking. His style on the mike was inspired by suave, if artificial-sounding, radio deejays like Frankie Crocker of WBLS, New York, who made his voice as deep and manly as possible and crooned, "I can't lose with the stuff I use. . . . " Kurt's signature rhyme went, "When Kurtis Blow is on the go, he's gonna make you hate your stereo/When Kurtis Blow is ready to rock, he'll make you tick just like a clock."

A month later Russ threw his second party, billing Kurt

with Eddie Cheba. This time it was given at the 500-person capacity Palm Room of the Hotel Diplomat, located just off Time Square in Manhattan. The Diplomat had been built in 1908 as the New York City home of the Elks Club, which was then opened to the public after World War II. The twelve-story structure was never a grand hotel, and you could still rent a room there in the late Seventies for $15 to $20 a night.

Parties at the Dip were fun, but the crowds tended to be rough. Various young gangsters and freelance "hard rocks"—as well as plenty of just plain teens—seemed to love the new music. They'd show up, get a little crazy, start a fight, pull out a gun or a knife, and break up the party.

More often, there'd be trouble outside the club. Just two doors down from the Diplomat was Xenon, an elite Studio 54-styled disco. Admission to Xenon was in the range of $15 per person, but you couldn't just *buy* your way in—you had to radiate a magical combination of money, good looks, connections, and some kind of hard-to-define "fabulousness" before you'd find yourself ushered inside by the doorman. That meant that there was always a crowd on the sidewalk of rich, sheeplike, would-be glitterati surging up against the velvet ropes blocking off the entrance to the club. Russ's patrons liked to rob the Xenonites waiting in line.

"We went through a lot of security companies," Russell said. "They worked one show and that was it—the next security company would come. The Diplomat had bullet-proof box offices. Kurt and I stayed back there for most of the night, and when it was time to go onstage, Kurt would run out and perform and then run right back."

Risky or not, Russell's parties were soon featuring all of the earliest stars of rap—Lovebug Starski, Grandmaster Flash &

the Furious Five, Grand Wizard Theodore and his crew of rappers . . . and DJ Hollywood. Hollywood is the man who invented the rhyme that went, "Hip hop, the hibby, the hibbity hip hip hop, you don't stop," which every rapper in the world used to borrow, and which—in the shortened form of hiphop—has come to stand for all of hiphop culture, including rap.

Flash was widely considered the greatest of the deejays, the "grandmaster" of two musical techniques unique to rap—scratching and cutting. Scratching was a new kind of percussion in which tonearms and turntables replaced sticks and drums. The deejay "played" two turntables and a mixer. While the first turntable was playing a record with a beat, the deejay, using his headphones and a mixer, would cue the record on the second turntable to a particular horn blast or drumbeat or shout or moan, catch hold of that record at its edge, and start up the turntable underneath. Then he'd "scratch" the record by moving it under the needle according to whichever rhythm he felt complemented the music coming off of the first turntable. Cutting was simply segueing from one record to the next without missing a beat.

"Flash could spin with his toes and around his back," remembers Dave Sims. "He had a routine with two other deejays where they were cutting with no headphones. They'd walk around in a circle, and each guy passing the turntable would reach down and cut, and the next would come by and cut, and they would never miss a beat." Flash was a show all by himself, but he'd often appear with the Furious Five emcees, or in tandem with the Five's great Melle Mel. And after Russell got into the business, Flash also performed on occasion with Kurt.

Pretty soon, Russ started putting on shows in Queens as

well as in Manhattan. The way Dave Sims tells it, competition from the rest of the party promoters and rappers in Manhattan was so fierce— and ugly—that he had no other choice.

"Russell really had to struggle because these guys were close-knit and they didn't want to share the wealth. They'd all struggled to get to a point, and they didn't want to give that knowledge to somebody new just so that he could be equal right away. They wanted him to struggle, too.

"So, they would spread rumors—'Hey, Russell's gay!'—that kind of stuff," Dave continues. "The partying community was very tight and a rumor like that could hurt a person. People would suddenly perceive you differently." Dave leans back in his chair and squints appraisingly, as if at this Simmons character he thought he knew. "Suddenly it was, 'Is there something else about this guy?'

"But no matter how hard they tried, Russell shot past them. Russell had that drive. He'd go introduce himself to people the other promoters had only heard of, and these people would pick up on Russell's vibes and his ideas, and they'd say, 'Hey, this guy is on the ball!'" Russ himself described the phenomenon more modestly: "Give a party, you find friends."

In Queens Russell had no time for anything but the music business and gave up selling reefer. Sometimes he'd promote two parties on one night, sometimes three in a weekend. "I always like to have it hectic like that," he said.

By the beginning of 1978, it was hectic enough that Kurtis needed a full-time deejay—and Russell knew just where to find one. His younger brother Joey, then 13-years-old, would fill the bill nicely. A carefree kid, Joe wrote a rhyme in 1986 that delivers a telling view of his youth: "I've never been deprived of nothing I like/As a kid I chilled hard, bag of chips and a bike." Elaborating later, he said, "The worst thing that ever happened to me as a kid was that gym class would run out of time and I couldn't play my basketball game. Oh yeah, I couldn't bring my radio to school neither. But that's it. No way was I brainwashed or hurt by being black. It's not like I never had any money. I always had money."

Joey had early on worked it out so that he could have the Block *and* the Corner. "I went to school every day but I was cool with everyone—the jocks, the bad guys, even the nerds," he says. "See, no b-boy really wants D's on his report card. So they respect a guy like me, who can be streetwise and down but still get A's in class. It wasn't like I was a sucker for not taking drugs or something. I could hang, play basketball, and be down with them, then go home and do my homework."

Joe was also into music, so he naturally followed Russ's adventures with a great deal of interest. "Russell and Kurt used to come in late at night from the gigs with a whole lot of money," he remembers. "I knew they were having a great time and I wanted to be with them."

To that end, he had been learning to deejay on a little system he'd set up in the attic of his parents' house, and Russ had been monitoring his progress. "We called Joey DJ Run because he cut so fast. He could catch air on 'Good Times!' Just the breath and then nothing!" Russ recalls with pride.

It was indeed no small feat. Joey would begin on one turntable with Chic's vocalists singing "good times," just that one phrase. Then he'd cut, on the beat, to them singing 'good times" on the second turntable—a maneuver he had about a second to accomplish. Then he'd cut back to the first turntable, and again back over to the second. Having mastered that little exercise, he next started *paring down* the cut—from "good times, good times" to "good, good" to "guh, guh" and finally to . . . nothing! Russ had watched in awe as his little brother's arms flew from one turntable to the next. He couldn't hear anything—Joey was *catching air*—but he certainly could see that Joey had talent.

And so was born "Kurtis Blow's Disco Son—DJ Run." "Being that there was Flash out there," Joey says, "I was *real* happy with that name—DJ Run!"

As it turned out, DJ Run was first called upon to demonstrate his skills as a rapper, not a deejay. "He wrote a lot of rhymes and talked a lot of shit right away," says Russ. "Joey was def." The junior highschooler's very first show was at the Diplomat, where he was paired with Kurt and with no less a talent than Flash himself on the ever-loving wheels of steel. "Kurtis would rap and then he'd let his son rap," Russell remembers. "And then Kurt would rap again."

Joey had rhymes to burn right from the beginning. "I'm DJ Run, son of a gun/Always plays music and has big fun/Not that old, but that's all right/Make all other emcees bite all night." By "bite" Run meant that the rhymes he wrote were so witty and original that other rappers stole them and claimed them as their own.

Kurt and Run were a good team. Joey even remembers Kurt deejaying while his disco son rocked a rhyme about the two of them: "Apple to a peach to a cherry to a plum/We won't stop rocking till you all get some/When we all get some, we still not done/And that's why they call us Kurtis Blow and DJ Run."

Pretty soon Joe fell into a routine. "I used to go every Saturday and give out flyers, then I would do my little thing, get off the stage and get some money, and come home early in the morning real tired, a little kid eating breakfast at the end of the night."

Dreamy as it sounds, the shows could sometimes get a little nightmarish. Joey remembers that at Le Chalet, a 700-person ballroom, and at the Fantasia, both in Queens, "People used to shoot guns all the time. It used to get hectic." At maybe three shows out of five, he says, there'd be shooting. "You'd hear a cap go off—*Pah!*—and everybody'd go running a different way. If I was onstage, I'd just put the mike down and step to the side. One day after a show, they were shooting outside of Fantasia, and Kurt and I both dove under a car."

Dave Sims, who used to work the door for Russ, remembers a show at Le Chalet when the gang he called the Don't Pay Crowd came by and circled the door. "These were friends of Russell who said, 'By law, we don't pay,'" Dave recalls. "So the guy I'm with reaches under his shirt, as if he's got a gun. All of a sudden I see nine guns pointing at me! And the guy I'm with doesn't even *have* a gun! But that's just Queens for you. Everybody has a gun. They don't pay. They don't respect nobody."

A few years later Run wrote a surprisingly innocent rhyme (immortalized on the record "Here We Go") about his life as a teen star: "Cool chief rocker, I don't drink vodka/I keep a bag of cheeba inside my locker/Go to school every day/On the side make 'em pay/'Cause I'm rockin' on the mike till the break of day."

Whatever the venue, Joe had a schoolmate friend stand out in the crowd with a tape recorder—holding the box up above his head and pointing it at the stage—to record each show, so that Joe could study it at his leisure and learn what had worked and what hadn't the night before. Late Sunday afternoons, after he'd slept, Joe would arrange to get together with his partner D so that D could study it, too.

D was Darryl McDaniels and he lived off of Hollis Avenue on 197th Street with his parents Byford and Bannah and his older brother Alfred. Byford McDaniels was born in Jacksonville, Florida, and moved to New York at the age of 18. He joined the merchant marine seven years later, saw the world, met Bannah, and settled down to work as a stationary engineer for New York's City Transit Authority.

Bannah was born in South Carolina. She moved to New York after high school, worked as a beautician and then as a nurse, and now works as a nursing coordinator at a hospital in Queens. She'd gone to private school as a child, and decided that both her kids would, too. Her husband agreed that it was a good idea. "It seems like in the Catholic schools there's more discipline," he said. "Whereas in the pubic schools everybody was wild and nobody was learning anything."

So Darryl was sent off to St. Pascal's elementary school, where the big, quiet, bespectacled youngster became an excellent student and did his duty as an altar boy. But it turned out that he *still* had to deal with those wild public school kids. "They used to come up to our school and take peoples's earrings and money and stuff like that. So when you walking home from school and you got your school uniform on, you're like a target for the public school kids, and they start chasing you. I used to walk home, and if I saw them at the store on the corner, I ain't going to the store. I'm'a go home, change my clothes, and *then* go to the store. So now I'm fitting in with the crowd."

Mostly, though, Darryl just didn't go out very much when

he was little. The artistically inclined youngster used to sit in his mother's clean living room, where every precious object is in its place, and look out the window onto the street, and draw and draw. "My brother and I had about a thousand comic books, and I used to draw the superheroes," he explains. "We had every issue of Captain America, every issue of Spiderman, every issue of Hulk, every issue of Iron Man."

"After the comic book phase," D continues, "I found out about this thing called football." He played a year in a local league, and spent his twelfth summer lifting weights, but he knew he was eventually going to Brother Rice High School in Harlem, where they had no team because "there's no room for a football field on the corner of 124th Street and Lenox Avenue."

So D took up basketball instead, joining a Police Athletic League team, and becoming reacquainted with a fellow ballplayer named Joe Simmons. He and Joe had attended St. Pascal's together from kindergarten on, but because they'd never been in the same class, they'd never become close friends.

"Back in the day all I wanted to do was play ball for a whole bunch of teams," Joe remembers. "That was the cool thing—ball. If you couldn't play, you wasn't down." D's father put up a hoop in the McDaniels' backyard, and suddenly Darryl and Joe were hanging out together every day.

The two quickly found out that they also shared an affection for rap. "I heard a tape by Flash and I wanted to be like him," D recalls. His folks gave him the money for two $12 turntables and a $50 mixer and for copies of "all these beat jams going around"—"Fantasia" by Cerrone, "Super Sperm" by Captain Sky, "Apache" and "Bongo Rock" by the Incredible Bongo Band. D added what he needed from his mother's livingroom stereo, and set up what he and Joe thought of as their "laboratory" in the basement his father had paneled. He replaced the spindle at the center of the turntable with a section of broken pencil, the better to facilitate the quick change of records. He taped quarters to the top of the shell of the cartridge at the end of each turntable's tonearm to make sure that the needle wouldn't jump when he and Joe scratched a record. And thanks to the paper disk he'd slipped between the turntable and the record, the turntable spun but the record didn't—at least not until D or Joe turned it loose.

They'd switch off, Darryl deejaying while Joe rapped, Joe deejaying while Darryl rapped. D taught Joey how to spin (using James Brown's "Funky Drummer"). Joe told D, "Start rapping!" Then, D remembers, "Joe got some *real* equipment for his birthday, so Joe's house was the place to be for the next three years, day and night, Christmas and Easter!"

It had to be the attic for D because his mother wouldn't let him go out to see any rappers in action, not even Joey. "Mom," he'd ask of the strict woman he towered over, "Russell's giving a party and I wanna go with Joe and them."

His mother was firm. "No, you ain't going over there. It's bad over there! Go watch tv with your brother, or go to sleep."

There was no possibility of appeal. Crushed but mute, big D would stomp up to his bedroom and start crying. "I hope she die!" he'd think. "I hope she get hit by a car!"

But alone with his friends in the attic, high on reefer and "Olde E" (Olde English Malt Liquor), D got to calling himself Grandmaster Get High, and later, Easy D. Too shy to perform in public, and not allowed to go out, he would write and "bust out" (rap) the most amazingly "vicious" rhymes ever heard. His self-transformation from Darryl

McDaniels—the obedient Catholic schoolboy who crossed the street to avoid the local bad guys—to fearless, boom-voiced Easy D was easily as miraculous as the transformation of Clark Kent into Superman.

Consider this early attic rhyme:

> I was walking down the street on a Saturday night
> When all of a sudden I started a fight
> I punched him in his eye and it swelled up
> Then I pulled out my knife and gave him a cut
> Then I pulled out my gun, shot him twice
> Dumped him in the alley with all the mice
> As the story goes on, needless to say
> When I'm coming down the street don't you get in my way!

Filling out the crew in Joe's attic were Butter Love and Cool T, Runny Ray, and Thiggs. Butter was known to his parents as Douglas Hayes. A very funny guy and a good rapper, Butter got around. He'd introduced D and Run, and would eventually introduce the two of them to Jam Master Jay. He would also team up with Cool T under the name the Hollis Crew to write and perform a great record called "It's the Beat," which came out in the summer of 1985, the last independently distributed Def Jam 12-inch single. Raymond White, a/k/a Runny Ray, ultimately went to work for his old pals as their roadie, and ended up playing himself—the young man whose murder touches off a drama of revenge—in the movie "Tougher Than Leather." In his attic days, Ray had a rhyme of his own, composed for him by Run and D: "Toot the horn, ring the bell, I am the man with the clientele/Ring the bell and toot the horn, and then you know that Runny Ray is on."

Many a time, after the crew had finished in the attic, they'd walk over to the alley nearby to play back the tape they'd made and rap some more. The alley, just in back of one of the few apartment buildings in the Hollis, was one of the neighborhood's great hangouts. Unfortunately, even the alley had its drawbacks. Emboldened by the Olde E, the guys would scream out their rhymes at the top of their lungs, which would inevitably excite the attention of the building's superintendent.

"Y'all got to stop that noise! Take that stuff someplace else!" he'd shout. When this tactic failed to move the crew, the super would come running around the corner of the building with sticks and guns. This tactic always worked, although even in retreat D liked to save the last word for himself. "Don't tell me to be quiet! Don't you try it!" he'd shout. "You know my rhymes are def—you can't deny it!"

Sweet high-octane Olde E was a magic potion in D's life. He wrote a rhyme about it while he was still in high school that's damn near a love song:

I got this rhyme that's more than real.
When you drink Olde English here's how you feel
You reach in the freezer for a forty-ounce
Or a 32-ounce—whichever counts
Then you feel each bottle for the one that's cold
It's gotta be cold when you're drinking Olde Gold
But you might take the one that's hot
Said you gotta get it hot—that's all they got
A dollar fifty-five that is the price
That's not too much if you wanna get nice
You pay your money, walk out the door
And you say to yourself you'll remember that store

You look around for a place to stand
With a quart of Olde English inside your hand
Crack the quart, put it to your lip
You tilt it slightly and take a sip
Now by now you should know the deal
Cause that one sip you already feel!

To this day D loves the stuff, and he knows why, too. "The whole thing was you would buy your Olde English instead of cocaine or speed or something that cost $25. It cost a $1.55 a quart," he remembers. "*$1.55,* man? You have $1.55! Get you some Olde English, you can stand on the corner with your boys. It's not like being a wino. It's not like getting drunk off liquor, where you can't think. Olde E just loosens you up. You stand there on the corner on a hot summer day with your fresh Adidas on, ice-cold quart of Olde English, chatting with your boys, and by the time you drink half of that shit, you be *nice* for the rest of the evening. You'll be laughing and it make you wanna rap! Drink a 40-dog and I wouldn't be able to shut up for the whole day and whole night—be rhyming all night, *loud,* everywhere I go. Everybody'd tell me, 'Yo, why don't you shut up! You been rhyming all night!'"

By that time D was dumping deejaying for emceeing. "Rapping was more fun than being a deejay for me," he recalls, "cause I could get on the mike and tell people how devastating I am."

When they got tired of the attic and the corner, Joe and D and the rest of the crew might make it over to Two-Fifth Park in Hollis. The city's parks were, and still are, the great incubators of rap in New York. Nobody worried about a permit; a deejay with equipment would simply set up, start cutting and scratching, and pass around the mike. By 1980 or so, the deejay running the biggest and best system in Two-Fifth Park, and cutting up the deffest beat jams, went by the name of Jazzy Jase. "In Hollis, Jay was like Fonzie," remembers Run. "He was the best deejay, and the man everyone in Hollis knew."

Neither accomplishment was an accident. Jason Mizell had moved with his folks from Brooklyn to Hollis as a ten-year-old in 1975, and realized right away that "for security reasons I needed everybody to be my friend." His half-brother Marvin, ten years older, was already out of the house. His half-sister Bonita, seven years older, was finishing high school. He'd picked up some street smarts in Brooklyn, but Queens was a whole new territory.

"My block, Two-Third, was the center of Hollis Avenue," he recalls. "On the corner of my block was where all the stores were at and everybody meets up. Two-Fifth Park was in my backyard. If I was going to the store for my mother, all the wild guys would be there, so I had to be their friend in order not to be scared of them."

Accordingly, Jay and his little friends decided to build themselves a reputation for fearlessness. "Back in '78 or '79 there weren't any more gangs, but if you were small, you still had people running up on you, tapping your pockets, see if you had lunch money," Jay says. "Me and my crew got robbed a couple times by the same guys we see out on the street. But then we said, 'Yo, fuck that, man! Tomorrow when we go to school, we gonna be *flashing* our little bit of money, and we *dare* somebody to come up on us and take it. If they want it, they gonna have to beat all four or five of our asses.'

"So the very next day the same guys come up on us and

ask us for some money, and we just cold dusted them off. It was a turning point. All of a sudden we have juice on this avenue. No one from around here can come in and do *nothing* to me. We were about 13."

By the time Jay was in the eighth grade, he had juice with a class consisting of the toughest kids in the school, including many who were several years older than he. By the time he was 14, he could claim, "I was the motivator. All the big guys would say, 'Where we going tonight?' Any event that went down, I was on that train and 15 guys would move with me."

Though he was hanging with the tough guys after school, Jay in school was always in "the smartest class, with the nerds and the suckers." These poor souls included Jeff Fluud, who was such a "brainiac" that he ended up skipping the eighth grade and going straight into the ninth. A few years later, Jeff would rap in the park as "King Ruler" of Two-Fifth Down, Jay's crew. A few years after that he'd write "Jam Master Jammin'" for Run-DMC's second album.

It was also in the eighth grade that Jay—"just to be different from the rest"—began to shop for clothes for himself and to develop the fashion sense that would eventually be introduced to the world by Run-DMC. "I had my black velour with a feather in it, and my black and white Adidas with the shell toe, my Lee jeans, and I thought about how my colors had to be coordinated," he remembers. He even took the care to be sure that his "nylons" (underwear) matched his shirt and the laces in his sneakers—although the time and effort involved in changing his shoelaces *every day* is what led to the practice of using *no* shoelaces. After all, he points out, "It matches—no shoelaces matches with everything!"

Jay's friends had a little saying at that time that expressed their optimism with regard to the new decade—and their place in it. "I'm a choice nigga for the Eighties," they would tell each other. Looking back on it, the former Jazzy Jase says with a smile, "I *was* a choice nigga for the eighties, for sure."

Still, it took a certain amount of guts even then to wear what Jay calls "the b-boy style." "I used to have to fight for my velour in the seventh grade when guys would try me for my hat," he recalls. He disagrees however with the notion that b-boy style is exotic. "I had my hat and my Adidas. I was in a band and I was composing songs. I wanted to have a nice pretty girlfriend, and I wanted to be cool," he says. "'B-boy' is just a word. I think it's always been around. Way back in the day I saw a lot of guys, black and white, who have the same feeling."

Indeed, Jay's passion for his gear recalls nothing or no one so obviously as Elvis Presley, "a real gone cat" who grew his hair and his sideburns long in the early Fifties when all his highschool classmates wore crewcuts, who shopped for clothes in Memphis's black ghetto and came out wearing purple pants with black stripes down the side, white buck shoes, and a pink sports jacket (and then got beat up by the football team for his daring)—and who recorded a song about three weeks after his 21st birthday called "Blue Suede Shoes" that let the whole world know just what his gear meant to him.

> You can knock me down, step in my face,
> Slander my name all over the place
> And do anything that you wanna do
> But, unh uh, honey, stay off of my shoes

Of course, as it had been with Elvis and rock & roll, some

of the older folks were sure that every b-boy was a criminal
and that you could ascertain as much simply by eyeballing
the clothes these kids wore. Indeed, an African-American
physician and playwright from Hollis named Dr. Gerald
Deas went so far in 1985 as to produce a little-known
record—a *rap* record—called "Felon Sneakers" in support of
his guilt-by-association argument that felon sneakers were
"the kind of sneakers worn by Rikers Island inmates." The
doctor was further convinced that "those who favor them
often end up stepping on their own social and emotional
growth and tripping out of the job market." DMC would
respond to that reasoning in "My Adidas" in 1986: "I wore
my sneakers but I'm not a sneak. . . . "

Jay confesses, however, that by the 8th grade there were
"members of my direct posse who had stopped going to
school and were doing little penny-ante crimes—petty theft,
jostling, pickpocketing. They didn't need the money. They
just wanted to do it. It was what their uncles did in Brooklyn.

"I wasn't involved with it," he says. "But I was around it
all the time—a lot."

One day when he was 15 Jay got a little too close to
the action and ended up paying a pretty stiff price. A
friend of his had ripped off the house of a doctor in
Jamaica Estates, near Hollis, and run into Jay a few
minutes later. The two of them suddenly found themselves
being chased by an undercover cop, who finally ended
up collaring Jay. "Kevin was a light-skinned guy with an
Afro, wearing blue and black," recalled the style maven.
"*I* was wearing green sweats, green sneakers, a green
shirt—money green! But they said it was me, so I got
caught."

Jay could have been turned over to the custody of his

parents, but he was too embarrassed to tell them what had happened. Instead, he told the cops that he didn't have a phone and ended up spending four days at the Spofford Juvenile Facility in the Bronx, which he remembers as "a jail for kids who can't go to Rikers Island because they're too young."

Several of Jay's friends had been in and out of Spofford, so he figured he knew what to expect. "This is how dumb I was," he recalls. "I said to myself, 'I'm gonna love it here. I'm gonna love someone bothering me. I'm gonna love the fights I get into. I'm gonna love it all.'" In fact, Spofford wasn't at all as fearsome as advertised. "It looked like school facilities," Jay says. "Pool table, ping pong, and basketball in the backyard." Moreover, the biggest, ugliest kid there turned out to be an older guy from Hollis, and he and Jay buddied up right away. And when Jay and some other "new jacks" beat a team of longtime inmates in basketball, he won himself new friends. "All in all, when my pops picked me up, I was really having a good time," he says.

Debriefed about the experience afterward, Jay told his mother, "I had a lot of fun, Mom." That was not was Mrs. Mizell wanted to hear. She repeated Jason's answer . . . and then she started to cry.

Connie Mizell must have felt as if she were at the end of her rope. Jay had been sparing his folks the details of his wilder b-boy adventures. "At school I was trying to be cool," he says. "At home I was another person, and it was a whole different feeling." Mrs. Mizell knew, of course, that "a lot of Jason's friends were trouble." But as independent as Jay was, she says she also knew, "I couldn't pick his friends for him." And whenever Jay's father asked him about his more questionable activities, it was always, "Nah, I ain't messing with nothing. I'm cool. I'm doing everything right, Dad, for real."

He had, after all, a tremendous amount of love for his parents. Connie Mizell, who moved to Brooklyn after finishing high school in 1953, is the child of sharecroppers from North Carolina. She spent ten years working in a drycleaning factory and raising two kids with her first husband. After her first husband died, she married Jesse Mizell, a social worker. She gave birth to Jason, and *then* started going to night school, where she earned two degrees, all the while working as an assistant teacher. She's now a first-grade teacher in Brooklyn and a very active member of the Hebron Baptist Church, also in Brooklyn.

So Jay had certainly not intended to provoke his mother. He thought she'd been worried about the way he'd been treated in jail, and his answer was meant to reassure her, not to make light of the whole experience. But when she started crying "that's when I changed completely," he says, "and when I got the idea that you didn't have to rob and steal to be the best and have the most juice. You could still be def without having to be negative at all. I had my deejay job at the time to keep my clothes up and my equipment up, so you couldn't get me near any kind of robbery. It seemed like the worst thing in the world to me."

Instead of crime, Jay began to concentrate on his music. He'd first got involved with music when he was about ten, learning drums and bass, and playing in different bands. Then, when he was about 13, "all of a sudden *the deejay* became the main attraction. He'd come to a party with a turntable and giant speakers and records. Everyone stopped wanting to be in a band and started spinning records instead. I had a turntable, my friend had a turntable, so all I had to do was buy a mixer. They had mixers for, like, $39. So my moms got me a mixer, and I started off like that."

Eventually, Jay would play at 192 Park, at the park behind Andrew Jackson High School (which he and Joey both attended), at Jamaica Park, and of course, at Two-Fifth Park. "Every hot Saturday I'd take the equipment out to my backyard, cut through the next backyard, and start making a party out in the park. I'd set up and the whole neighborhood livened up. Run and DMC would come along and get on the mike while I scratched."

In fact, D claims *never* to have rapped in public, but he certainly used to hang out in the park with Run, and he remembers the scene with crystal clarity: "It's five o'clock on a summer day and everybody's in the park—the ballplayers and the college kids are out, the girls are coming and going, people are walking their dogs, the ice cream man is out there, the deejays are playing radio music, and the people across the street ain't mad at nobody.

"And then, as the basketball players go home, the *crews* come—you know what I'm saying? This is when shit gets wild. You probably see someone you had a fight with in school and start beefing, everybody's drunk and high . . . *and that's when it's mike-rocking time!*"

Jam Master Jay cuts in: "There were *so* many emcees out there in the house waiting for the mike! The mike is just going all around. There could be as many as three mikes, and all the emcees are trying to rap at the same time. Except for D. Everybody used to be, 'Take the mike, D!' 'Nah, D don't take the mike.'"

These rap parties in the park would "go until two o'clock in the morning, and if the neighbors didn't call the police, somebody'd start shooting and everyone would go home," says D. "It would happen almost every time. 'Oh, you was in the park last night? They started shooting again! Dudes was climbing the fences. Broke the party up.' Next week we'd all be back until 2:30 come—*bang! bang!*—everybody run on home. It was ill."

TWO

It's Like That

Ill it might have been, but Darryl and Joe and Jay were getting drawn deeper and deeper into the rap scene—and the schoolwork of all three began to suffer as a result. Joey was not only gigging every weekend, he was cutting school during the week to go home and practice his scratching. By the eleventh grade he was so far behind that he had to take night school to make up credits he was missing. Jam Master Jay, a year behind Joe at Jackson, ran into problems of another sort. By the time he was 16, he was "the big brother of the whole school." He knew and was friends with everybody—the athletes, the nerds, the brainiacs, the wild guys, the musicians, and the school's one white pupil. The school had hired a large security force to patrol the corridors, and the administration often employed Jay—who'd sworn off crime—as a peacemaker whenever a fight broke out.

One day he intervened on his own when he saw the Five Percenters, an offshoot of the Nation of Islam, hassling a couple of younger students, and was punched in the face for his trouble. When Jay's whole posse, unbidden, came to school the next day to avenge this insult—"When I got hit it was, like, 'Oh! They stepped on Hollis Avenue by hitting Jay!'"—his friend Hurricane, fighting with a Five Percenter in the hallway outside the classrooms, ended up getting shot in the leg.

Shortly thereafter, Jay decided he "couldn't take the pressure no more," and dropped out. He earned his Graduate Equivalency Diploma during the course of the next year, and spent a lot of time in the house taking care of his father, who was very sick and who would die in October 1982.

Even DMC, who'd been an A student his whole school career, finally started messing up, probably, he says, "because I was hanging out too much. I never failed, but I got a D in trigonometry and my mother got mad at me."In fairness to D, Rice wasn't quite the sanctuary Mr. and Mrs. McDaniels imagined. True, says D, "you couldn't wear sneakers, you couldn't be late, you had to shave, you had to do your homework." But "there were a lot of crazy motherfuckers from Harlem at Rice. Kids used to bring guns to school. A lot of drug dealers went there. Kids in my class, in the tenth and eleventh grades, were driving BMWs to school. No, they weren't selling the drugs in school. They were *taking* the drugs in school."

All three guys were out of high school by the spring of 1982 and enrolled in college that fall—although none of them was quite sure why he was there. Run enrolled at LaGuardia Community College in Queens as, of all things, a mortuary science major. "I was just a confused guy out of high school who could rap good," he recalls. "I figured if people was gonna be dying and all, I might as well get paid." The future, in truth, looked pretty grim. "I just thought I was going to get a job at Woolworth's right next to the college, eat lunch, go to school, come home, do my little homework, and not know what the fuck I'm gonna do."

D and his "ace boom bobby" Butter, with whom he'd gone all the way through school, from kindergarten on, decided to enroll at St. John's University in Queens as business majors simply so that they could stay together. "And then," he remembers, "I found out I didn't like it." More enjoyable were ROTC and his English class, where they studied the Greek classic "The Iliad," which D recalls was about "how all the gods, Zeus and them boys, went to war." He also remembers sitting in the cafeteria with his friends, beating on the tables and rapping. "We'd draw a lot of attention," he says.

Jay was more enthusiastic about higher education than his future partners. "I was proud to be a college student," he says. "After high school I was on that I-need-to-know tip." He enrolled at Queens College, where they invited the 17-year-old to pick a major out of a list of 20. "It was like 'Pick a number,' he remembers. Jay chose computer science, although he knew, "I wasn't gonna *be* in computer science. I was gonna take philosophy the next semester."

He recalls being "kinda scared" in the beginning. "I thought when I first walked in that somebody's mother was gonna be sitting in the back there. But it was just a bunch of kids like me, so now I'm relaxed." *Real* relaxed. The school was about 80 percent white, ten percent black, and ten percent "other," and Jay remembers being "the only serious b-boy in college—wearing suits, with a doo-rag hanging out of my velour, and my Adidas with no shoe strings.

"The teacher was like, 'You think if I came to work dressed that way, I'd still have a job?' I said, 'If I was a professor, I wouldn't come to school dressed like this. Your main problem should be me learning the work. Ask me about the homework.' I had the street in me. I was hungry to win, and I wanted to be the best in everything."

By this time Joey had been nagging Russell for several years to make a record on him and his crew. Russell'd been initiated into the record business in 1979, when a couple of *Billboard* reporters named Robert Ford and J.B. Moore pooled their resources to produce a rap record about Santa Claus in Harlem. Scouring the New York scene for a suitable rhymesayer, they settled on Eddie Cheba—until Russell talked them into working instead with Kurtis Blow.

Writer Nelson George, who was on the scene at the time, is convinced that "Russell's presence was as important as Kurtis's talent in convincing Robert and J.B. that Kurt was the one. Russell was the only young guy on the rap scene who seemed to have any long-term goals. He was serious where his contemporaries just wanted to party. Everybody wanted to make records. But did everybody realize what promotion and marketing to the nonrap audience would entail? Did they realize that if rap was successful they'd be approached by record industry pros, people who didn't give a fuck about anything except their ability to make a quick buck? Russell did."

"Christmas Rappin'" came out in time for Christmas of 1979, following by a few months the first huge hit rap record in history, the Sugarhill Gang's "Rapper's Delight." It was a hit, and Kurt followed it up in the fall of 1980 with "The Breaks," which was a much bigger hit. The twelve-inch versions of both records have since gone on to sell over a million copies.

For all the success of Kurt's records, however,

Russell—who was now formally managing Kurtis—was not knocked out by their pop oriented production style. He wanted to make "beat" records, records that were faithful to the sound of rap as it was being heard in the city's clubs and parks, and at his own parties. But it wasn't until he teamed up with Larry Smith, the bass player on "Christmas Rappin'" and "The Breaks," that Russ found someone who could translate his ideas to vinyl.

Larry Smith had grown in St. Albans, Queens, which borders Hollis, and attended Andrew Jackson High in the same class as Danny Simmons. He'd been hooked by music at a young age, spent a lot of time watching the great acts of the Sixties at the Apollo, and then taught himself how to play bass by listening to James Brown's records.

He got his first steady gig while he was still a high-schooler, as a member of the house band at an after-hours spot in Bedford-Stuyvesant in Brooklyn, a place he recalls as "a hustler's paradise." He went on to tour with a blues singer from Alabama who ran a barber shop in Brooklyn during the week. He played with the Brighter Side of Darkness when he lived in Chicago for a while. He did all kinds of session work, played punk-rock and jazz, and, when he returned to New York City, weddings and bar-mitzvahs, too. Later, Larry went to Albany, where he led the pit orchestra in a production of "Your Arms Too Short to Box with God." In 1978 Larry moved to Toronto, where for two-and-a-half years he acted and led the house band in a jazz musical called "Indigo."

Home for Christmas in 1979, he ran into his old friend Robert Ford. "Rocky was the first person I ever met who didn't work, but who made money," says Larry with undisguised admiration. "So I had to grow up and be just like him." It was Robert who hired Larry to play on Kurtis's records. Russ and Larry first collaborated as producers on a record by Larry's band, Orange Krush, called "Action," which featured vocals by a hot young singer named Alyson Williams. Then they collaborated on a funky and funny rap called "The Bubble Bunch" by Jimmy Spicer, both of which came out in 1982. These were influential jams, but the labels involved didn't promote them, and they didn't become hits. (Sugarhill Records put out an "Action" rap by the Treacherous Three which, Larry claims, "used our beat straight up," but without giving any credit or payment to its originators.)

By Christmas of 1982, Larry and Russ, trying to figure out the next step for Orange Krush, decided to make a rap record. Russell's first idea was to ask a hip and attractive white Englishwoman named Blue to team up with Joey and Davy D—the great Queens deejay who had replaced Joey in Kurt's act when Kurt hit with "The Breaks" and had to start touring widely. They would call this line-up the OK (for Orange Krush) Crew. "Disco was still kicking us all in the backside," Larry remembers, and Russell hoped that Blue's presence would "strengthen the alliance" she'd already begun to assemble as the booking agent for a rollerskating rink on Manhattan's far west side that doubled as a nightclub called the Roxy. Blues's policy was to book rappers, which meant that uptown rappers and downtown rockers—a potentially powerful alliance indeed—were getting together on a regular basis for the first time.

The OK Crew never came to pass. Joey was determined not only that he'd make a record, but that when he made it, it would be with his partner DMC.

Joe's determination had been strengthened a couple of months earlier when, as a solo act, he cut his first, abortive, record. Trevor Gale, the drummer from Orange Krush, had written a rap song called "Street Kid," and then approached Russ looking for a rapper. "No problem," said Russell. "I've got just the person for you. Joey will be perfect." In truth, Russell says he let Joey cut "Street Kid" because "I didn't care. I wasn't planning on making Run-DMC records. But Joey kept bugging me to make a record, so. . . . It's funny. I didn't have enough belief in my own brother. I knew how good he was, but it just didn't occur to me that he could be a star."

Musically, "Street Kid" is not at all a bad record—but the attitude is dead wrong. Trevor and his wife Chyna wrote the original lyrics, which were then customized by Joey, who placed the action in Hollis and named off members of the Hollis Crew. It is a mildly pissed-off complaint about being dismissed as a "hood" because he dresses with "my hat turned around, my pants leg down"—that is, like a b-boy. The song concludes with, of all things, a plea to the old folks for understanding: "Adults out there, we've all got brains—Why don't you treat us like you oughta ?"

The arrangement is thoughtful, with a swirling keyboard line propelled by a hard spare drum beat, a funky bass, and a deep, Vocoderized voice singing the refrain.

Then 17-year-old Run, sounding very young, starts rapping:

> While chilling on the spot the other day, just thinking to
>   myself
> You see I wrote this rap just to tell you all just exactly how
>   I felt
> I went to Hollis Ave. just to see who's there
> People judge us by how we look and by what we wear
> My man Darryl Mack thinks it's all a joke

But me myself I think it's wack 'cause I'm a cool-out folk.

Trevor shopped around the demo to all the major labels but found no takers. "They were all scared of rap then," he explains. "Street Kid" by DJ Run never saw the light of day.

Now that Russell and Larry were serious about making a record with him, Joey's first task was to convince them to let him make it with D. But whatever Russ's doubts about Joey, he was sure he didn't like D. D and Russ had been arguing for years, whenever they saw each other over at the Simmons's house. "I always thought Kurtis Blow was corny and I told Russ so," D remembers. "The Funky Four was the aggressive niggers I wanted to be. That's why Russell didn't like me—'cause he had Kurt, and Kurt was getting the money: 'This is what it is right now.'"

Russell remembers it a little differently. D was such a devoted fan of the music, and such a reliable barometer of a record's value, that Russ used to test out new Kurtis Blow records on him. "He'd sit there with his hood up and rock back and forth and sort of shake his head if it was good," Russ recalls. "But when Kurt was making records that were more commercial, D would sit there and listen and not shake his head. Kurtis and I would look at him and say, 'Oh shit! We're not going to sell any records!"

To show him the kind of rap he *did* like, D would recite some of his own rhymes, which *Russell* didn't like. "It's too hard. It's too aggressive. It's not commercial," he'd say. Joey would immediately jump up in Russ's face. "You dummy!" he'd scream at his older brother. "D's the best rapper in the world!"

Then Joe had to spend some time convincing D himself of that, too. "It's a visionary thing with me. I see what I want and I get it. Long as you fight for what you see, you can have it. With D I used to break out in a stupid sweat and tell him he's the greatest king of rap that's ever been."

Joe also had a vision of just how to proceed when it came time for him to make his first real record. He'd had the rhymes that would become "It's Like That" for a long time. In fact, he'd sold an early version of them to Larry for use on a Kurtis Blow record. Larry paid Run $100, but Kurt never recorded them. (Although he had used some lyrics by Joey on "Got to Dance," which came out on Kurt's *Party Time* EP in 1983). "It's Like That" began, "Unemployment's at a record high/People coming, people going, people born to die/Don't ask me 'cause I don't know why/It's like that. . . . "

One day, remembers D, "We were in a movie theater in Manhattan. We snuck in and we're sittin' in the girls' bathroom 'cause the boys' bathroom was messed up. And Joe was telling me, 'Never take your glasses off again.' I thought glasses were square. I used to wear 'em in school and take 'em off and put 'em in my book bag when I left school. But Joe saw me wear them with my Kangol and he thought it looked good."

Joe continues: "I said, 'We gonna make this motherfucker, and we gonna make a movie' . . . and he was gonna do it with his glasses on. He felt like he was a sucker if he put them on. So I said, 'Your glasses are cool. Your glasses are the most b-boy incredible thing you could ever do to yourself! Put the motherfuckers on. You're gonna see your way home, and you'll make these goddamn rhymes.'"

D had already written a few lines that fit Joe's concept in his English class, where the students were given five minutes at the end of every session to write or draw in a "log book." The rhyme went: 'You should have gone to school, you should have learned a trade/But you laid in the bed where the bums have laid/Now all the time you're crying that you're underpaid. . . . " At home he sat down and wrote fifteen more pages of lyrics.

Run and D have worked together in this fashion ever since. "I'm Chief in Charge of All Ideas," says Run. "D's no subject maker. He's like the guy who needs a frame before he can paint a picture. Once I come up with the idea, D goes and starts writing a lot of stuff toward it."

One day after school Run and D took all their rhymes over to Larry's place in South Jamaica. Larry and Russ were up in the attic, where Larry had a little recording studio—and where he'd devised a radically new arrangement for a rap record. Most of the top rappers at the time—The Sugarhill Gang, Grandmaster Flash & the Furious Five, the Treacherous Three, the Funky Four Plus One, Spoonie Gee, the Crash Crew, Busy Bee, and others—recorded for Sugarhill Records, which was owned and operated by the husband-and-wife team of Joe and Sylvia Robinson. Joe took care of the business side of the label, while Sylvia ran the creative side.

Sylvia herself went way back in the record business. She had made hit records as one-half of Mickey and Sylvia in the Fifties, written and produced great street corner ballads by the Moments in the Seventies (they went on in the Eighties to make hits as Ray, Goodman and Brown), and scored a significant pop hit on her own with an ultra-sexy item called "Pillow Talk" in 1973. It was also Sylvia who produced the Sugarhill Gang's "Rapper's Delight." The record was released as a 12-inch single, but people got their money's worth—that one song was 15 minutes long. Sugarhill claims to have sold 6.5 million copies of "Rapper's Delight." It's the kind of achievement that can go to your head, and by 1981 Sylvia was calling herself the Queen of Rap and showing up at parties dressed as Cleopatra.

Sylvia's productions for her rappers were tough and funky, but they featured a live studio band with a horn section, a sound that nothing to do with the actual sound of rap as it had been made for years in the city's clubs and playgrounds. "Those arrangements were bullshit," Run now says. Ever the competitor, his only thought before he himself actually got into a studio was, "If *I* could be down, I'd be a lot better: Imagine a young rapper making a record, *this* young, with *this* voice."

Larry understood, and had created a track that left plenty of room for vocals, featuring little more than a drum machine smashing out a stark beat, dressed up just a bit with the occasional synthesizer swoosh and sting. Up in Larry's attic studio, Russ looked over D's lyrics and then parceled them out, assigning some lines to D and some to Joe. And then D had one more idea: "After we say, 'It's like that . . . ,' we ought to say, ' . . . and that's the way it is!'" And Russell said, "All right! We got a record here!"

At the time "The Message" by Grandmaster Flash & the Furious Five was the biggest rap record in the country. It featured Melle Mel in the strongest and scariest performance of his career, rapping in great detail about life in the ghetto and the pressures that come with it. The refrain paints a picture of a Travis Bickle-like young man a hair's breadth from exploding:

Don't push 'me cause I'm close to
The edddddge!
I'm try-in' not to lose

My head
Uh huh-huh-huh-huh!
It's like a jungle
Sometimes I wonder
how I keep from going under.

Joey was likewise interested in reaching his peers with a message but, unlike Mel, he would not include snapshots of "rats in the front room, roaches in the back." "I just thought I'd tell people what the world is like, and how to improve themselves," he recalls. "It wasn't optimistic or pessimistic; it's just like that, and that's the way it is. It was a pep talk for the kids that was also good dance music, to keep them on the right track." The strategy marked the group as serious artists, and because the lyrics weren't specific to life in the ghetto, all kinds of people, not just other ghetto kids, could relate to them.

The b-side, "Sucker MC's," started out as a "bonus-beat" throwaway—but it turned out to be at least as influential as "It's Like That." Jam Master Jay, in retrospect, understood that as well as anyone. "There was never a b-boy record made," he said, "until we made 'Sucker MCs.'" Run, dreaming of his first record, had imagined "nothing but hardcore, b-boy, wizard, winning shit. Def b-boy stuff, like we used to do in the parks—just straight-up scratching over a beat, rapping."

Larry accommodated. His arrangement this time was even sparer than the one he'd concocted for "It's Like That." Essentially, he programmed a drum machine to duplicate the beat pioneered by Trevor Gale on "Action"—Buh-boom *bap*, bap boom *bap*! Buh-boom *bap*, bap boom *bap!*—and added handclaps. It was a beat that could stand up to the best Russell had ever dug as a youngster.

And the introduction Larry devised was just as great. A fanfare of drumbeats like gunshots—boom *bap bap bap bap bap!*—set up a dancer's expectations, and then the beat itself dropped like a bomb. But when it came time on the record for D to rap, the drums dropped out altogether and the beat was scratched in, another innovation. "We were selling vocals," Russell recalls. "We figured we had very, very good rappers and we wanted people to appreciate what *they* did. We didn't want to overproduce them. Of course, Joey and D wouldn't let us play music anyway, just wouldn't let us. We'd say, 'Put in a little melody here, a simple melody,' and they'd say, 'Absolutely not!' Turned out they were right."

The song was eventually subtitled "Krush Groove 1," and for good reasons. First, it was the groove originally designed by Larry Smith of Orange Krush for their record "Action." Secondly, it was not just *any* groove, it was a *crushing* groove. This is also why the name of the record label in the movie of the same name is Krush Groove—those were the kind of records the label made. (The same kind of hopeful poetry, by the way, was at work when Rick Rubin named his record label Def Jam—all the jams he and Russell released were def.)

The opening lyrics to "Sucker MCs" were first conceived as part of a rhyme by D about himself and his friend Joe. (In the following lines, "black" is a kind of very potent marijuana, "Hard is Hard" was a club in Harlem on 125th Street, and "OJ" is a deluxe gypsy taxi cab, an Oldsmobile or a Lincoln or a Caddy.)

Two years ago a friend of mine asked me to say some emcee rhymes

So I said the words I'm about to say. The rhyme was def
and it went this way:

Took a test to become an emcee, and the President became
amazed at me

So they put me inside a Cadillac, the chauffeur drove off
and we never came back

Went uptown to buy some black, because the Hard is Hard
is not the wack

Then we went to the store to buy some beer. The chauffeur
drove off and left me there

So I went to the phone to call a cab. I didn't have a dime.
It made me mad

So I asked this girl for a dime. The girl was fine. She was
so divine

Then I called the OJ from the phone. Up pulled a car with
the light green tone

I got in the car. So did this freak. We got so high that she
kissed me on the cheek

Went to her house. I paid and got out. What happened
that night y'all know about.

Russell's main plan for "Sucker MC's" was to recycle the
"Action" beat. He cared less about the lyrics. "Just be sure to
mention Orange Krush and tell 'em where you go to school,"
he said to Run. Given that much freedom, Run came up with
something brand new in rap—an attack on other rappers, a
straight-out "dis," which is short for disrespect. If you dis
somebody—bump into him at a club by accident and take
too long apologizing, look too hard and long at his girl,
whatever—then you're looking for a fight.

Like D's rhyme, Joe's begins with him taking a test to
become an emcee, but then, following Russell's instructions,

it wasn't the President who "became amazed", but Orange
Krush.

> . . . So Larry put me inside his Cadillac, the chauffeur
>   drove off and we never came back
> Dave cut the record down to the bone, and now they got
>   me rockin' on the microphone
> And then we're talking autographs, years of laughs,
>   champagne, caviar, and bubble baths
> You see, that's the life that I lead and you sucker emcee,
>   this is who I be
> So take a' that and move back, catch a heart attack, because
>   there's nothing in the world that Run will ever lack
> I cold chill at a party in a b-boy's stance, and rock on the
>   mike and make the girls want to dance
> Fly like a dove, they come from up above, I'm rockin' on
>   the mike and you can call me Run Love.

The first part of that verse is pure autobiography: Larry is
Larry Smith and Dave is Davy D. But all that business about
champagne and caviar is just standard b-boy boasting. In fact,
in the life Joe led then, and in the life he continues to lead,
he cares nothing about those things. What he did, and does,
care about is rapping. Now here comes the dis:

> You're a five-dollar boy and I'm a million-dollar man
> You're a sucker emcee and you're my fan
> You try to bite rhymes, all lines are mine
> You're a sucker emcee in a pair of Calvin Kleins
> Coming from the wackest part of town, trying to rap but
>   you can't get down
> You don't even know your English, your verbs or nouns
> You're just a sucker emcee, you sad-faced clown

After a short and snappy introduction by Run—"So, DMC, if you're ready, the people rockin' steady, you're driving big cars, get your gas from Getty"—D raps the rhyme he'd written especially for the occasion. Like Run's, it was autobiographical. Like Run's, it was about rap and rappers above all. And like Run's, there was a lot in it that was new for rap: a fresh combination of the intellectual (the emphasis on the value of a *college* education) and the earthy (the description of his favorite soul foods), and the proud confession that he was from Queens, of all places. . . .

I'm DMC in the place to be. I go to St. John's University
And since kindergarten I acquired the knowledge
And after twelfth grade I went straight to college
I'm light-skinned, I live in Queens, and I love eating
 chicken and collard greens
I dress to kill. I love to style. I'm the emcee you know who's
 versatile.
All my rhymes are street delight, so here's another one for
 y'all to bite
When I rhyme I never quit, and if I got a new rhyme I just
 say it
'Cause it takes a lot to entertain, and sucker emcees can be
 a pain
You can't rock a party with a hip and a hop. You gotta let
 'em know you'll never stop
Your rhymes have to make a lot of sense. You got to know
 when to start when the beats commence.

D recalls that Russell got very excited after D first tried that rhyme out on him, exclaiming, "I never knew you could rap like that! I never knew you could rap like that." Then, says

D, "I was *souped!*" How great it was to have Russ appreciate his talent after having argued with him for so long.

Run-DMC had a rough demo now, but they needed something of studio quality if they were going to make a record deal. And so Larry and Russ placed a call to Greene Street Recording, in the chic Soho district of lower Manhattan. Greene Street was their home studio, the place they'd cut all of their records, beginning with Kurt's "Christmas Rappin'."

When J. B. Moore first met Steve Loeb, the studio's then 28-year-old owner, Greene Street was notable as the site of sessions by John Lennon, Ornette Coleman and Phillip Glass. "We were," Loeb says, "inclined toward offbeat artists." Loeb found himself bowled over by the enthusiasm of J.B. and Rocky for this new rap stuff. "It was like religion to them," he recalls.

Now Roddy Hui, the Hong Kong-born house engineer, called Loeb into the studio. Larry was on the line, playing him the demo of "It's Like That," and Roddy put it onto the speakerphone for Steve to hear as well. "I thought it was great," he remembers, and ended up advancing Larry and Russ the $3700 they needed to record "It's Like That" and "Sucker MCs." Of course, by that time, having known Russell for years, Steve thought of him as "the most amazing promoter of all time," and probably would have advanced Russ the studio time even if he hadn't liked what he heard over the phone.

Now the crew had a good-sounding demo, but they didn't have a name. Russell suggested Run-DMC, which combined the name Joe had performed under for years with the one D had made up for himself in typing class his last year of high school. (He's said on record that it stands for "Darryl Makes

Cash" and "Devastating Mike Control," but DMC started out as nothing more illustrious than an abbreviation of his full name, Darryl McDaniels, to DMcD, which he then shortened even further to DMC.)

At first, D recalls, "We were saying, 'Please don't call us that! Please don't call us that!' It sounded so crazy weak and retarded. But after awhile, after we heard it on radio, it began to sound better. Now you can't help but say Run-DMC and it's def!"

Russell took the demo of the songs around to all the major record labels and found no takers. One might have predicted that he'd have had trouble selling such raw music to older white record executives, but Russ also found that none of the *black* executives at the majors wanted anything to do with Run-DMC. "They're bourgeois blacks," he explains. "They don't understand it. It's not sophisticated enough for them. They're looking to sign up Peabo Bryson again and again. It's also *too black* for them. Rap reminds them of the Corner, and they want to be as far away from that as they can get."

Russell finally visited Profile Records, a tiny independent label run by a couple of white guys in their middle-20s named Cory Robbins and Steve Plotnicki. They'd started the company in 1981 with $34,000, put out a few disco records that went nowhere, and six months later were down to their last $2000. They spent $750 making Dr. Jeckyll & Mr. Hyde's "Genius Rap," released it in 12-inch form in November of that year, and sold 150,000 copies. That one record, a rap record, saved the company.

Cory thought the demo of "It's Like That" was "pretty good," but not "unbelievable." "I thought it was good enough so that, if they weren't asking for a tremendous deal, we would take a shot at it," he recalls. "Originally Russell came with one price and I said, 'No. We'll do it for half that money.' And he said okay. We would've just let it go otherwise, because we had no idea. We just thought it was another good rap record." And then, four or five weeks later, "it exploded and started selling 20,000 copies a week."

Run was walking down a hallway at LaGuardia Community College in April of 1983 when he first heard "It's Like That" on the radio. "I went runnin' up to this guy with his box, screaming, 'That's my record! That is *my* record!' He believed me. He had no other choice. I was ecstatic."

D informed St. John's that he'd have to take a leave of absence. "And," he says with the most satisfied of smiles, "I've been absent ever since."

THREE

Here We Go

Jazzy Jase was real mad. Here it was, the night of the biggest party he and Two-Fifth Down had ever thrown, a going-away bash for his crew's own DJ Nellie D, who was moving to Texas, and it looked as if the whole of Hollis was there—except for Run and D. Not only that, Jay knew where they were and what they were doing, and he was mad that he couldn't be with them.

He cooled off a little the next day when they came around with a tape of "It's Like That." Run had always promised Jay that when he made his record, Jay would be his deejay, and now he was keeping his promise. Run and D and Jay began practicing together, getting ready to go out on the road.

That very first day, cementing the new partnership, Run made sure Jay was there when it was time for Run-DMC to pose for their first pictures as a group. They're pretty revealing, those shots. It's obvious that Jay is the one with the most developed idea of b-boy style, and the strongest commitment to it as well. There he stands in the middle of the trio, his hands on his belt framing the gold "JAY" buckle, wearing a black leather bomber jacket, a black leather cap, and a gold "JAY" nameplate on his chest.

Run's maybe halfway there. He's wearing a leather jacket. But his Lee jeans are white, not black, and his hair is wrong, an Afro with sideburns, instead of the close-cropped b-boy style. D is wearing an ordinary cloth trench coat, looking more like a garden-variety college student than like a rapper. Obviously, he hadn't yet moved on the resolution he'd made years earlier, when Butter first introduced him to Jay. "Jay just had to be hip," D remembers. "He had all the def stuff, the sneakers and hats, that I didn't have. I thought, 'Man, I want *all* of this!'"

He'd have it soon enough, in time for Run-DMC's first night of gigs. They were coming up fast, and included a performance at Disco Fever in the South Bronx. Between 1978 and 1985, when it was shut down by the police, the Fever was the world capital of rap, an after-hours spot for teens located a subway stop away from Yankee Stadium in the heart of America's most famous slum. Ronald Reagan, touring the scorched surface of the South Bronx as a presidential candidate in 1979, was inspired to hark back to his wartime adventures. "I haven't seen anything as bad as this since London after the Blitz," he said.

But if the kids of the Bronx didn't have much else in the way of cultural or economic advantages, they did have the Fever. It wasn't a large place, but most nights 600 to 700 kids would squeeze into the club's second story, with the first floor handling the overflow. Opened at midnight, things didn't really start heating up there until 2 a.m. or so, at which point they would cook away until eight in the morning, when the diehards were finally pushed out, squinting, into the daylight and onto the street.

The only trouble was getting in. The five-dollar cover charge was no big deal at all, but every patron not only had to walk through a metal detector at the front door, he had to face a pat-down by Mandingo just the other side of that door. Mandingo is an extremely solid six-foot, five-inch gentleman who was very thorough about his job. Consequently, there was generally a long line of kids waiting to get in, a line that snaked all the way down the block of Jerome Avenue on which the Fever stood.

Mandingo disarmed any number of prospective patrons during the night, but occasionally someone would get through with a weapon, which meant that occasionally there was serious trouble. The threat of such trouble never seemed to faze the club's regular clientele. Newcomers troubled at the sight of this entry ritual, however, were soothed by the honeyed advice of Sal, the club's owner, who always told them, "Don't be scared. Feel safe!"

The second floor was the scene of most of the action. Coming to the top of the steps, one saw a large horseshoe-shaped bar to the right, and a little photo concession to the left (manned most nights by the short and energetic Mr. Lloyd Nelson), where for five dollars the club's visitors could get good-looking Polaroid snapshots of themselves and their dates as souvenirs of their visit to the Fever.

Just beyond was the dancefloor. Dimly illuminated from above by a perimeter of red marquee-styled lights, it could accommodate maybe 300 dancers, and often had to. At one end of the dancefloor was the stage, about 25 feet wide and ten feet deep. On the wall behind the stage was the club's famous backdrop. In fat red graffiti-styled letters a foot high, it read, DISCO FEVER, THE HOME OF . . . and, in white letters against the black background in the spaces around the name of the club, it proceeded to spell out the monikers of the stars of rap: KURTIS BLOW, GRAND MASTER FLASH, JUNE BUG, HOLLYWOOD, SWEET GEE, STARSKI, KOOL KYLE, STARCHILD, SUGARHILL GANG, SEQUENCE

Beyond the dancefloor was another bar, quieter than the one up near the door, and off that bar was the back room (called Part Four), where the Fever's preferred clientele would retire to consume their illegal refreshments.

Opposite the stage, at the back of the dancefloor, were the private offices of owner and operator Sal Abbatiello, the 30-ish Italian-American who'd had the inspiration to transform one of his father's failing salt-and-pepper bars by instituting a music policy—namely, rap—that appealed to a younger and larger crowd.

Sal is of medium height, lean, dark and good-looking. He used to stroll the Fever wearing a gold chain around his neck from which hung a golden crown inscribed "King of Disco Fever." In an interview in 1983 he said, "My white friends say, 'Why you stay over there?' I say, 'Why not? White people got guns, too.' I'm not white, and I'm not black. I'm an American, I'm a New Yorker, and I was born in the Bronx. I've been doing this all my life. I did it when this was a white neighborhood, but everybody ran. I stayed."

The pride of the Fever was its state-of-the-art deejay booth, up above the bar, and it was from up in the booth that house deejays like Lovebug Starsky and June Bug usually worked. As a rule, the Fever did not hire a lot of outside talent to perform for its patrons. Rather, in addition to the entertainment provided by the deejays—and by singing emcees like Sweet Gee and Ronnie DJ—the Fever sponsored regular weekly events in which the club's clientele themselves provided the entertainment. Every year for weeks at a time the Fever would run in-house versions of "The Gong Show," "Name That Tune" and "The Dating Game," as well as a bathing suit contest—all of which awarded cash prizes to the winners.

The Fever was self-contained and it *worked*. It was also the place where many of the city's rappers—at least those from the Bronx and Harlem—ended up at the end of the night, whether or not they'd had a gig. Much more than a disco, the Fever was, in Sal's formulation, "The YMCA of the Bronx." Kurtis Blow, for example, used to go there six and seven nights a week. "It was like home to me," he said. "I could go to the Fever and act like a fool and I wouldn't hear about it later." And this was *following* Kurt's stint as one-half of the regular Tuesday night team at the Fever—his partner was Grandmaster Flash—a gig he held down for $20 a night from the fall of 1978 through the spring of 1979. If he were forced to, of course, Kurt could justify his constant hanging out at the Fever as *research*. "It's where I get ideas for my album," he said at the time. "You get to see what the street likes."

Russell, naturally, had been friends with Sal for years, and had even worked for him on a freelance basis promoting records that came out on the Fever label, like Sweet Gee's "Games People Play." Russ also religiously brought test pressings of his new records to the Fever's deejays, with the knowledge that if a record pleased the Fever Believers, then he could be pretty sure that it would please kids like them throughout the country. The converse was also true. "If a record won't go around in the Fever, it's fake," he swore.

The Fever Believers could always be counted upon to do their part when it came to making a party a *party*. Up in the booth, Starsky might be cutting up the hypnotic funk that comprises the first eight bars of Michael Jackson's "Beat It," and then, with the entire dancefloor heaving beneath him, he'd open the mike, and shout, "What's that word when you're bustin' loose?"

"Juice! Juice!" the crowd would shout.

"And how do you feel when you got that juice?"

"Loose! Loose!" they'd roar back. And right on beat, too.

Jay and his Hollis Crew homeboy Randy had checked out the Fever as budding 15-year-old party promoters. Looking around in amazement and approval, they told each other, "Yeah, this is the way *we're* gonna do it." Two years later Jay looked forward to Run-DMC's debut date at the Fever with intense anticipation. "I always wanted to be on the stage at the Fever," he recalls. "I was going to be happy to go in their deejay booth and show them what a kid from Hollis Ave. can do. I knew their turntables were better than the ones I was using 'cause Larry was always bragging about their turntables. So I was going to go the Fever that night, and I was going to be the total b-boy, and I was going to *win*."

He'd made his arrangements the day before with Larry, Run, and D to be picked up at his house at six o'clock on the night of the show. Larry, who'd performed the same duties for Kurtis (at the time he was also leading Kurt's band), was now pressed into service as Run-DMC's road manager. "I was *hooked* this day," Jay remembers. "I had a black leather suit, a pair of 'didas with no shoestrings, with a black velour *that day*." In other words, Jay had assembled Run-DMC's

"King of Rock" outfit nearly *two years* before the release of *King of Rock.*

Unfortunately, Larry left Hollis with Run and D at four-thirty that day, and forgot Jay. Jay couldn't believe it. He paced back and forth, from the living room to front porch, wondering what the hell had happened. When Larry finally called to tell him they'd gone to New Jersey to do the gig they had to do before they got to Disco Fever, Jay was crushed. He knew he'd never be able to make it over there in time, and that he'd have to miss the gig. He hung up the phone and cried.

Run and D's first show that day was an after-school affair at a club called Lola's. "It was for all these old . . . *office* people," D recalls with distaste. "I remember everybody was wearing gowns and suits." Afterward, Russell yelled at the two of them because they hadn't moved onstage *at all.*

In fact, it would take a few months before Run-DMC got their stage routines together, but on that night, for that show, they were additionally hampered by the fact that there was only one mike for the two of them. This might not have been such a big deal if the two of them had worked in the style established by groups like the Furious Five, where one rapper recites his whole rhyme, and the second his, and the third his, and so on. But from the very beginning, with "It's Like That," Run and D had begun alternating not just verses, but lines. The speed of these exchanges was dazzling, but with only a single mike at their disposal, D was forced to hover next to Joe when he was rapping, so that D could grab the mike in time to say his line, and then pass it back again.

The awkwardness at Lola's was just the beginning of what would turn out to be a pretty long night for Run and D. "When we walked into the Fever wearing the crazy checkered jackets, everybody just started laughing at us," D remembers. "Then when they found out who we was, there was a big beef: 'These kids from Queens trying to cold crash the rap scene!'" Run and D were dressed, at Jay's suggestion, in one of his classic getups: plaid jackets, white pants, black and white Adidas with the shell toe (although D was wearing Pumas).

They started to make up lost ground when they hit the stage, starting with "It's Like That." "They didn't like us preaching to them: 'You should have gone to school! You could have learned a trade!'" recalls D. "But we was doing it *mean,* pointing niggers' *faces*! Then when 'Sucker MCs' came on . . . "—he sings the opening drum fanfare—" . . . it was like, *'Owwwohhh!!!* That's the jam!'"

Still, at the end of the night D went home mad. "I'm gonna take *all* these kids out!" he vowed to himself. He wrote a rhyme that ended up on "Jam Master Jay," the b-side of the group's very next single. It is not only a bold announcement of the arrival of Run-DMC, it turned out to be a devastatingly accurate prophecy regarding the fate of their predecessors:

> We're live as can be, not singing the blues. I got to tell you all the good news
> The good news is there is a crew. Not five, not four, not three, just two
> 'Cause it's about time for a brand new group. Run-DMC will put you up on the scoop
> We make the fly girls scream in ecstasy. We rock the freshest rhymes at this party
> We put all the fellas in a daze. It's everyone that we amaze. . . .

"I was talking about the Furious Five, the Fearless Four, and the Treacherous Three, telling them that we taking over," said D. "And that's when the Five broke up, that's when the Fearless Four broke up, that's when the Treacherous Three broke up—and ever since then we just been *ruling*."

A year later, after the original Furious Five had indeed broken up, no less a rapper than Melle Mel answered both "Jam Master Jay" and "Sucker MCs" on a song called "The Truth."

> From around the way, back in the days, we got beat so you
>   could get paid.
> We made you a job, you two-bit slobs. Now you don't have
>   to work, to learn, steal or rob.
> You got a *little* bit of fame and wealth. Now you think you
>   did it all by yourself, hah!
> I am you, but ain't me, because you didn't start rockin' till
>   '83.
> Melle Mel is the best that will ever exist—and if I gotta be
>   a sucker, suck on this!

Much of Mel's anger is understandable; rap is extremely competitive, he'd been number one for a long time, and suddenly and rudely he'd been knocked out of the box by these young upstarts. But that crack about Run-DMC not having started rocking until '83 is not only unfair, it's untrue, as Mel well knew. How many years, after all, had he played on dates with the Son of Kurtis Blow?

In any case, Jay later put the Bronx versus Queens controversy into perspective. "The feeling inside of me was never a soft feeling," he said. "It's no matter where you're *from*. It's who you *are*. There's no difference between the Bronx and Queens. It's just that we live in houses and they live in projects. So what? They went outside and had a fight with the guy down the block. We went outside and had a fight with the guy around the corner. No difference. Everything that was everywhere else was in Queens, too."

Very soon this kind of beef was academic. By May 1983, "It's Like That" was getting played on black radio stations from one coast to the other, and Run-DMC—Jay included—had to hit the road. They weren't making a lot of money—Russell sometimes had them play for free, just to get them some exposure—but they sure were making a lot of friends. In the New York area they might do as many as four shows a night: a "shorts and t-shirts party" at a roller rink in Queens called the United Skates of America; The Club Ecstasy in Brooklyn; the Wheel (another roller rink) in New Rochelle; and finally the Fun House in Manhattan (where they would be recorded performing "Here We Go" on August 5 of that year).

Soon enough they were gigging outside the city, traveling in Larry's light blue '78 Cadillac Coupe DeVille, a roomy and powerful hog that was just right for the job. D remembers fantasizing that the four of them were stick-up kids. "Larry's the driver, and we put on our black suits and our black hats and go around sticking places up. While we onstage, distracting the people, Larry's in the back *getting money!* We used to come home with stacks of cash every night!

"And then we was on the move: 'We be waiting for you tomorrow, Larry.' Larry come get us and we back on the road. Go to *Boston*, Larry used to do ninety! Pull up at the club, get the turntables out, go set up, kick ass, get back in the car, shoot down to *Connecticut* . . . and we was doing that *all night*! That's when we were having fun with Larry. We was rolling!"

A few months down the road they had to fly as well as roll, to get to gigs down South as the opening act on bills with Cameo, the Gap Band, the Barkays, the Dazz Band, Zapp, and Midnight Star. Once again, D remembers it well. "We used to go out onstage and bust they ass! After we finished, the crowd don't want to see these jerks jumping around with Jheri Curls, singing and playing the drums."

Why not? Well, maybe it was because Run-DMC's stage show was just as radical, and just as rootsy, as their records. Essentially, all they did was adapt to the stage a typical Saturday night rap session in the park. To begin with, they had no band and they had no instruments. They had a one-man band, and his name was . . . *Jam Master Jay*. That's right, the deejay who only weeks before had been known throughout Hollis as Jazzy Jase had been redubbed Jam Master Jay, the Big Beat Blaster by DMC, who also immediately began writing rhymes about his new partner. Like this one: "He's Jam Master Jay, the big beat blaster/He gets better 'cause he knows he has ta/In '84 he'll be a little faster/And only practice makes a real jam-master."

It was a rhyme that would show up on their next single, "Jam Master Jay," which opened with the material that Jay quickly adapted to ignite Run-DMC's live shows. They kicked off each show the way DJ Run had begun his shows with Kurt, with the deejay calling out the star with his turntable. Alone on the stage, Run would scratch up a line from one of Kurt's records—"Now I'm the guy named Kurtis Blow! *Kurt-Kurt-Kurt-Kurt*-Kurtis Blow!"—and the man of the hour would take his time and then amble out, and finally grab the mike, and demand, "What's my name?" And the well-primed crowd would scream—what else?—"Kurtis Blow!"

Now it was Jay who started out alone onstage, standing behind a table holding two turntables and a mixer, scratching out, "*J*-A-Y are the letters of his name! J-J-J-*J*-A-Y are the letters of his name!" Then he would start scratching, "D! D! D! D-D!" for fifteen or twenty seconds, revving up the crowd's expectations, and finally letting the whole phrase play—"D-M-C!" And suddenly there he was, in person, big D onstage with a mike in his hand. He'd hold one arm up over his head, his palm facing the crowd, and momentarily calm the commotion. "My man Run wants to come out and play for y'all, but he thinks y'all ain't live enough," he'd announce solemnly. "Y'all wanna see Run?"

And of course the kids would scream, "Yes!"

And D would say, "All right then. . . . Lemme hear you say, 'Ruuuuuun!'"

And the crowd screamed, "Ruuuun!"

"Say, 'Ruuuuun!'"

And the crowd screamed "Ruuuuuuun!" even louder than before. Then Jay cut in on the beat, scratching, "Run! Run! Run! Run-Run!" even longer than he'd scratched out the letters of D's name. And as he scratches, finally here is Run himself, his head down, striding onto the stage. He walks up to the mikestand, slowly unhooks the mike, grabs the mikestand by the throat and hurls it violently into the wings, raises *his* hand and screams, "Now it's about that time for us to say that we're . . . "

And for the first time Jay plays in its entirety the phrase he's been worrying to death for the previous five minutes: " . . . *Run-DMC and Jam Master Jay!*"

It really didn't matter which town they were in. By this

time the crowd was wild with excitement—and the show itself hadn't even properly begun. And then it was on to "Sucker MCs" and "It's Like That"—with D and Run stalking the stage from left to right and back again, D busting his rhymes to the rafters, Run often running up on D and screaming his rhymes into D's face—and they'd end up *slaying* whoever else was on the bill. And the recipe was so simple and tidy. "No instruments needed, just two record players/A stage, a crowd, and two rhyme-sayers," as they'd lay it out on "Jam Master Jammin'."

Still, not an easy act to follow. Small wonder, then, that the nominal headliners usually fixed it so that they *wouldn't* have to follow this trio of ass-kicking 18-year-olds onstage. After suffering a couple of public humiliations, the tour's top-billed act invariably went around to talk to the promoters privately, and next thing you know one of the backstage guys was poking his head into the crew's dressing room and announcing, "Run-DMC's going on last tonight." And the guys would look at each other and then back at the backstage guy and wonder, "Word?" Says D, "We felt *big* then."

Of course, it wasn't only their music and their stage presence that made Run-DMC so unbeatable. As the first real black *rock* stars of their generation, they didn't care too much about dressing up for the stage in the style of the older groups. As critic Richard Grabel noted in a review of one of the crew's shows at New York's Danceteria: "Not for them the street punk-meets-'Blade Runner' costuming currently favored by the Furious Five, or the Spacemen and Indians pow-wow of Soul Sonic Force. They'd rather be ordinary homeboys in street clothes who hit you hard with the news they're bringing. They don't need smoke bombs. They've got verbal bombs to drop."

All three of the guys remember an intimate little style war with the Fearless Four at a club in New Jersey shortly after Run-DMC first hit. The Four were from the Bronx and, as they were then gigging locally behind the success of the Kurtis Blow-produced hit, "Problems of the World," they ended up on a lot of shows with Run-DMC. "We used to come to our gigs dressed in jeans, ready to tear shit up," says Run. "And the Fearless Four always had these leather suits on and white boots and their hair braided." Run recalls the night when the Four couldn't resist commenting on Run-DMC's choice of stage apparel. "They said, 'Man, y'all come just like y'all come off the street!'" I said, 'That's how we comin', boyee. That's how we livin'! Goin' out like b-boys, *troopin'*, not goin' out like a roach, like the rest of you soft-assed rockers, boy."

The crew's decision to "dress down" in "street clothes," instead of "up" in leather and chains and fur, in the style of the older Bronx rappers, was made very consciously. After listening to tapes of Grandmaster Flash and the Furious Five for years, D saw his first live show by the oldschoolers in 1984. "I was so disappointed," he recalls. "These ain't the guys I was always worshiping! They came out dressed in their braids and shit. Corny! I thought, 'Don't you know? You're *Grandmaster Flash*, you knucklehead! You're supposed to *be* him! What are you doing dressing like this and disappointing me?' But that just gave me the confidence to think, 'Fuck it! Me and Joe and Jay are gonna set an example!'"

Rick Rubin, the white producer who would team up with Russell to co-produce Run-DMC's *Raising Hell*, says that he thought that when Run-DMC dressed down, it was "just like white kids who can afford new jeans wearing ripped jeans. Black kids used to have to dress up as a status symbol. Now b-boys dress like gangsters as a status symbol."

The question of hair, meanwhile, was so important that the crew eventually wrote a rhyme about it. On "Rock Box," DMC raps, "No curls, no braids, peasy hair, still get paid"—a reference to hair so curly that it balls up like a pea on the back of the neck, which is another way of saying "bad" hair. Standing up for such a natural style was a mark of race pride. It was also a signal to their fans that Run-DMC were not, in Run's words, "out of reach." Or as Jay put it, "When people seen us, they seen that we was regular normal people who didn't go around with no braids in our hair, flicking them around. People tend to like what's real. And we was real."

It all comes down to *image*. Russell, as a manager, has always said, "We don't make records, we build artists." He means that the history of pop music is littered with one-or-two-hit wonders, and that one of the ways you increase the chances that your artist will stick around for awhile is to help him create an image for himself that's more enduring than any one record. Russell's beliefs chime in with those of the Rolling Stones: "It's the singer, not the song."

What that has meant with regard to Run-DMC's clothes is Russell making sure that they all wore more or less the same gear onstage after a while—black velour Stetsons with black leather suits and white laceless Adidas during the winter, Adidas warm-up suits and terry-cloth Kangol hats when the weather got warmer. By the time *King of Rock* was released in January 1985, the guys could put out an album cover that showed very little more than their iconic hats and their eyes (with D sporting his trademark glasses)—and everybody cruising the aisles in the local record store *knew* that it was Run-DMC's newest album. In other words, they'd created an image as memorable as Michael Jackson's sequined glove, or ZZ Top's beards, or Madonna's belly button.

But it wasn't just any image. It was, says Russell, an "outlaw" image. "Run-DMC is not for the Bill Cosbys. People talk about how there aren't enough black role models on television, but what they mean is there aren't enough *white* black people on television. Cosby's great, but he doesn't represent all of black America. If you're a black American, your neighbor is more likely to be like my artist Oran "Juice" Jones than like the Huxtables. And Run-DMC is something else again. They talk directly to the kids. What we're talking about is kids from middleclass families acting out street fantasies."

Russell couldn't have been more perceptive about television's uneasiness with the b-boy image, as was demonstrated by the weird tribute paid to Run-DMC by CBS-TV's "The Jeffersons" in the fall of 1983. The most popular black sitcom in history until "The Cosby Show," "The Jeffersons" charted the comic complications of a black family's having "moved on up to the east side." The greatest gift the Jeffersons' new social position had brought them, apparently, was the freedom to act as goofy as their white neighbors.

In this episode George, who is by day the owner of a drycleaning operation, has been talked into managing a group of singers with showbiz ambitions. The group is called the Satin Sisters and they are played by Sister Sledge, the real-life pop music hitmakers. George has no idea what he's doing, and books them by mistake into a redneck bar in New Jersey. Discovering upon their arrival just how far away they are from their neck of the woods, George tries to play it off, saying, "Uh, I think you girls should start with 'I'm Glad to Be an Okie from Muskogee.'" Once the laugh track subsides, George and the cowboy owner decide it's time for a little heart-to-heart talk.

Owner: This ain't gonna work.
George: What are you talking about? Music is music—
         ain't no black and white in entertainment.

So the cowboys, with grave misgivings, let George have his
way, and Sister Sledge hit the stage . . . and perform *"It's Like
That!"* They've changed around the words a little, and
worked out a Las Vegas-styled dance routine to go with it,
but the sisters look as *bad* as they've ever looked, and when
they finish—having shouted out, "It's like that! And that's
the way it is, *huh!*"—they end up with their fists in the air in
a four-across black power salute! The cowboys sit there as if
they're made of stone and George flips. He leaps up onstage
from a ringside table, makes with a big phony laugh and,
Tomming away at 90 miles an hour, assures the cowboys,
"They didn't mean that, folks." Turning back to the girls, he
whispers, "Are you crazy?!" Facing the audience again, he says,
"Just a little tribute to Charlie Pride . . . and now we start the
real show."

Now, of course, the cowboys want no part of the Satin
Sisters. Once again, George has to convince the head cowboy
in charge that these girls are all right, give 'em just one more
chance, etc., and once again the cowboy reluctantly relents.
Rushing back, the sweat streaming off his brow, George
motions the girls to try again. The sweet young things are so
disheartened, however, that they just don't want to go through
with it. George puffs himself up, sternly reminds them that this
is their "big chance," and says, "Let your music speak for you."
He starts to return to his table, but halfway back twists around to
the girls and spits out of the side of his mouth, *". . . and none of
that militant stuff!"* The Satin Sisters come immediately to their
senses and launch into Stevie Wonder's "Always" and their own
"We Are Family," neither of which, by the way, remotely recalls

Charlie Pride. This being television, however, we find the whole bar clapping and dancing along as the credits role, the picture of racial harmony and happiness.

Even more telling, when Run-DMC approached the producers of "The Cosby Show" itself in an attempt to get booked, they were denied. The most popular show on television in the Eighties, which happens to have an all-black cast, "The Cosby Show" refused to book the most popular of America's black teen musical acts.

One time, however, Run-DMC and the teenage members of the Cosby clan did manage an end-run around square old Papa Cosby, whose taste in musical guests runs to pop instrumentalists like Grover Washington, Jr. Run and the crew met Malcolm Jamal Warner, who plays Theo Huxtable, on a set that duplicated his "Cosby Show" bedroom on NBC-TV's "Friday Night Videos" on October 18, 1985. The sketch began with the crew surprising Theo in the middle of a telephone conversation. They then played him the "King of Rock" sequence from "Krush Groove," the movie that was just about to premiere. Clip concluded, we return to Theo's room, where foxy young Denise (Lisa Bonet) has just stormed in, demanding to know why her brother hasn't introduced *her* to the crew.

Run-DMC has had their real-life battles with the black middle-class, too. Larry Smith recalls the crew often returning to their hotel rooms immediately after shows down south not just because they wanted to—as they sometimes did—but because many times, their work for the night done, they'd try to visit one of the local discos and get turned away at the door. "Sorry, fellas," the man would say, "no sneakers allowed."

Of course, when their album came out a year later, and fans who hadn't seen them live had their first good look at

Run-DMC, they had to be pleased. The black and white cover shot by Trevor "Butch" Greene shows Run and D with their backs to a brick wall. They're dressed in Adidas warm-ups and their velours, and D is wearing his glasses as well. They are not smiling. D is leaning into the camera, and Run is pointing his finger straight into your face. Above their hats is RUN-DMC in jagged orange letters against a clashing pink background. In sum, they looked just they way they were *supposed* to look, the way that b-boys across the country had *hoped* they would look. "That's when we were in our prime," D recalls proudly. "We knew we were the baddest b-boys around."

Speaking of image, Run was once asked if the crew ever thought of themselves as sex symbols. "No!" he replied. "We don't care about being sex symbols. We're not rhyming to be adorable. We're rhyming to be devastating."

And right on cue, DMC bellowed, "Which we are!"

FOUR

Laying Down Law From State to State

The crew toured all summer and into the fall of 1983 on the strength of "It's Like That/Sucker MCs," which eventually peaked at number 15 on *Billboard's* Black Singles chart—not too shabby at all for a debut effort, and remarkable for a debut effort by a rap group on an independent label. Still, one twelve-inch single does not a career make, so Run-DMC released "Hard Times/Jam Master Jay" in December.

"Hard Times" is Run-DMC's remake of a song that first appeared on Kurtis Blow's 1980 debut album on Mercury, although "remake" doesn't really do justice to the transformation the crew worked on the original. Kurtis's version—lyrics co-written by Russell, music co-written by Larry—is a very funky, swaggering, James Brown-styled record in which Russell and Larry had both been disappointed. The problem is that its lyrics are talking hard times, but the arrangement and Kurtis's vocals are talking paaaaarrrrrrty!

So Russ and Larry combined the song's lyrics and the "Action/Sucker MC's" beat (which is why it's subtitled "Krush Groove 2") and came up with a worthy successor to "It's Like That." And though Run and D are rapping essentially the same lyrics Kurt had, their delivery is much harder and much more sincere-sounding. The opening verse paints a picture of economic desperation:

> Hard times! Spreading just like the flu. Watch out, homeboy, don't let it catch you
> Prices go up, don't let your pocket go down. When you got short money you're stuck on the ground
> Turn around, get ready, keep your eye on the clock, and be on point for the future shock.
> Hard times!

> But by the last verse, the crew has turned the gloomy picture into a pep talk:

> Hard times can take you on a natural trip, so keep your balance and don't you slip
> Hard times is nothing new on me. I'm gonna use my strong mentality
> Like the cream of the crop, like the crop of the cream, beating hard times that is my dream
> Hard times in life, hard times in death, I'm gonna keep on till my very last breath.

"Jam Master Jay," as mentioned, is the crew's song of praise for their one-man band, and it is also the record Jay himself used to open their live shows. And like "Sucker MCs," it is a b-side that is more exciting than the A. The pairing bulled its way up to number 11 on the Black Singles chart in March 1984—Kurt's version had stalled at number 75—by which time the crew was already working on what would become their first album.

Actually, Larry and Russ were doing the lion's share of the work. All that fall and into the new year they assembled Run-DMC's first album, which would be released as *Run-DMC*. They had set up shop, as usual, with engineer Roddy Hui in Greene Street's modern, brushed cedar-and-glass studios, and worked out most of the arrangements before Run and D ever stepped foot in the door. At the time Run and D didn't like spending time in the studio. They'd run in, cut their vocals to the tracks composed by Larry and Russ, and run out again—unless they hadn't managed to finish writing their lyrics in the car on the way in from Queens to Manhattan, in which case they sat down in Greene Street's lounge and wrote there. And the musician in Jay had yet to win his due respect, so he likewise spent very little time in the studio.

But Russ and Larry had cooked up a pretty ambitious plan. The typical rap album then consisted of a hit single or two and a lot of filler. Production-wise, the trend was simply to recycle somebody else's work—Chic's "Good Times," the Tom Tom Club's "Genius of Love," Taana Gardner's "Heartbeat," Queen's "Another One Bites the Dust," and others. Run-DMC's debut album would break the mold: nine songs, all of them originals, and every one a winner. It included, to begin with, all four of the songs that had been released and proven as singles. Then there was "Hollis Crew," which contains what has turned out to be Run-DMC's most enduring and generous pep talk, the one that invites kids everywhere to identify with the group and their success: "Now the things I do make me a star, and you can be too if you know who you are. . . . "

"Wake Up" is the story of "a wonderful dream" about "a vision of a world working as a team." And that's not all:

> Everyone was treated on an equal basis, no matter what color, religion, or races
> We weren't afraid to show our faces. It was cool to chill in foreign places
> There were no street people, we lived rent-free, and every single person had a place to be
> A job, a home, and the perfect pay, and the world was free of greed and hate.

It was a bold dream but, as the disturbing chorus keeps reminding us, "it was *just* a dream. . . . "

The lyrics to "30 Days" were co-written by J.B. Moore, who'd co-produced Kurtis from the beginning, and by Daniel Simmons, Russ and Run's father. The funniest song on the album, it's about "a man with a guarantee"—"and if you find that you don't like my ways, then you can send me back in 30 days." It would be the fourth single released off *Run-DMC* and the third to break into the Black Singles Top 20.

"Jay's Game" is a virtuoso cut-and-scratch workout by the Jam Master, the equivalent on *Run-DMC* of Grandmaster Flash's great "Adventures on the Wheels of Steel."

Of course, as a producer, Russell's approach has been to stay away from whatever's typical. And the least typical, which is to say the most innovative, song on *Run-DMC* is "Rock Box." True to its title, "Rock Box" features a grinding, heavy-metal guitar part, one of the very first records by rappers to do so. (The notable predecessor was the Treacherous Three's "Body Rock" from 1980, which had employed thunderous Hendrix-styled guitar to stunning effect). Then again, Russ has always insisted that what makes a record rock is nothing so obvious as a guitar—it's the beat and the attitude.

But one day Run-DMC was at Greene Street, waiting for a hard-rock band from Brooklyn called Riot to finish up so that could get into the one studio. "They saw these loud guitars," remembers Russell, "and they started screaming, 'We can do that! What the fuck—we're going to make loud shit, too!'"

Steve Loeb, the owner of the studios, remembers talking to Larry at the time. "Every time he mentioned to me this idea of a rap/heavy metal crossover, I would say, 'You're out of your mind! How could you possibly do that?' And Larry would reply, 'Niggers play rock'n'roll, too.'" Or as Russell said, "Rap is the outlaw black music, and rock is the outlaw white music. Two opposites together as one."

Ultimately, Larry got in touch with Eddie Martinez, a guitarist friend of his from Hollis. They had known each other for years and had played together in rock bands in the mid-Seventies. Eddie had gone on to play with Labelle and Nona Hendryx, and, shortly before Larry called him, he'd been on the road with Blondie during their last tour (a gig that Larry had tipped him to). He's since played sessions with everyone from Mick Jagger and David Lee Roth to Chaka Khan and Bootsy Collins. Larry played Eddie the rhythm track he and Russ had cooked up, and encouraged the guitarist to riff his way into heavy-metal ecstasy—which he did, with great glee. Martinez later said that Larry then multi-tracked his part. "I'd say there are close to ten guitar tracks on there," he recalls.

The lyrics to "Rock Box" are once again along the lines of "Sucker MCs," although Run does take the time to make a rhyme in defense of b-boy fashion: "Calvin Klein's no friend of mine/Don't want nobody's name on my behind/It's Lee on my leg, sneakers on my feet/D by my side, and Jay with the beat."

Russ had Profile release "Rock Box" as the crew's third single in March 1984. "At first black radio didn't know what the fuck it was. They liked everything else on the album better," he remembers. "But they tried it for us, kids called the stations requesting it, and 'Rock Box' became a hit in those markets. So then Run was free to try new things—and the only thing that's going to hold back any artist is a lack of creativity."

Though "Rock Box," was accepted by black radio (it peaked at number 22), it did not cross over to the Hot 100. That important piece of business—recognition by the huge white record-buying, rock-loving public—would begin to be accomplished thanks to MTV's warm welcome of Run's first video. Directed by Steve Kahn in black & white, the video of "Rock Box" begins with a speech by Professor Irwin Corey, "the world's foremost authority." An older comedian who's been around forever, Corey's shtick is learned-sounding double-talk. In the video the bug-eyed prof babbles away unconvincingly about the similarities between rap and the fugues of J.S. Bach until he's mercifully pushed off the screen by the disbelieving glares of Run and DMC. As the beat drops, we cut to a Caddy limo pulled up in front of a club. In an appropriation of the old circus trick, dozens of Run-DMC's friends and associates climb out.

Cut to Run-DMC on stage at Danceteria (then a very popular and hip downtown rock club), rapping to a houseful of all kinds of young people, rappers and rockers, black and white alike. Their first lines are delivered directly into Corey's face: "To all you sucker mc's perpetrating a fraud/Your rhymes are cold wack, keep the crowd cold bored/You're the kind of guy that girls ignore/I'm driving a Caddy, you're fixin' a Ford. . . . " And so it goes. At the end of the piece, they slap hands with a shy young white kid who's watched the action from the wings and, with a wink to the camera, walk out into the night.

MTV played that video all summer long. At the time the channel played very few videos by black artists of any stripe, and they'd never before added a video by rappers to their regular rotation. But "Rock Box" fit MTV's format—or at least it was closer to their racially-restricted idea of rock than videos by such other popular black acts as, say, Rick James or the Gap Band. Of course, it would be two more years before America's rock radio stations (which to this day maintain a policy of strict racial segregation) would loosen up sufficiently to play any of Run-DMC's records. And even then, presented with the crew's release of a remake of Aerosmith's "Walk This Way"—a certified rock radio classic—it was the rare, shockingly daring rock station that gave it a chance.

The rock *critics*, however, loved "Rock Box" from the start—even as Russell, for one, found their enthusiasm amusing. "I didn't think 'Rock Box' *meant* much until I read some reviews," said the record's co-producer. "Rock critics make something out of everything." In fact, the critics were right on the money. Greg Tate acclaimed it as "nothing less than a staged confrontation between hip hop and heavy metal." Roy Trakin, writing for *Creem*, described it as "a searing rap rocker with a rumbling metallic guitar solo from Eddie Martinez that does for hip-hop what Eddie Van

Halen's run did for Michael Jackson—bringing it to a whole new audience." Even *Rolling Stone* sat up and took notice, praising the track for "melting rap into rock like it's never been done before."

The critics, in general, along with the more adventurous college kids of the day, were very enthusiastic about Run-DMC, which was important given the resistance the crew faced from both rock radio and black radio. Following the release of the album on March 27, 1984, Robert Christgau, the self-appointed "dean of American rock critics," declared in the *Village Voice* that *Run-DMC* was "easily the canniest and most formally sustained rap album ever." Frank Rodriguez, writing for *Splash*, the arts magazine of the Ivy League's Vassar College, took the crew out of competition with other rappers and set them up on the world stage—"In today's pop landscape of megastars with sequined gloves and perfectly coiffed limeys with arty but empty ditties, Run-DMC's message and sound have an aural punch that is more than interesting: it is vital." For that matter, the limeys themselves liked it. Richard Grabel, reviewing a May 1984 show at New York's Danceteria for England's *New Musical Express* wrote: "They've got the timing, they've got the tricks, they've got the tracks. . . . But most of all they've got the headlines and the street news flashing like a very quick teletype in every line. No banners waving, no big deal emphasis on it, but these raps tell true tales about all kinds of crises, economic, social and personal."

At about this time the crew was introduced to rock'n'roll face-to-face by Lou Reed. Reed is a very literate New York-style rocker who first surfaced in the mid-Sixites as the leader of a band called the Velvet Underground under the sponsorship of pop artist Andy Warhol. He'd had a few pop hits, notably 1973's "Walk On the Wild Side" (a loving reminiscence of the freaks in Warhol's crowd), but his subject matter was generally far too raw and too downbeat for radio. He sang in a Bob Dylan-influenced monotone about drugs, sex, music, and what people do for money and fame.

In the summer of 1984 MTV asked Reed to host a show devoted to New York rock as part of a series they were running called "Rock Influences." As host, Reed insisted on choosing his own guests, and if his choices had almost nothing to do with what was then fashionable on MTV, they nonetheless reflected his deep appreciation of New York rock's past, present and future.

His list included Arlene Smith and the Chantels, a great rock vocal group who'd had their first hit in 1957; Jim Carroll, a gaunt, red-haired, Reed-influenced rocker and author who could have been billed as the Son of Lou Reed; Reed himself . . . and Run-DMC.

As far as Reed was concerned, Run-DMC were strictly in the tradition of New York's street-corner vocalists. "Their lyrics are grown-up doo-wop, doo-wop with humor and social consciousness, zooming right into the Eighties," he said. "They're a perfect example of what people can do with imagination, energy, a drum machine, and a ton of talent."

Reed's generous endorsement, however, was not enough to guarantee the crew a warm welcome when they taped the "Rock Influences" special in front of a live audience at the Capitol Theater in Passaic, New Jersey on September 25. (The show would air on October 10). An all-white crowd, these kids were growing up culturally-deprived, attending segregated suburban schools and listening to segregated rock radio. Even so, most of the three thousand or so kids present that day listened with interest to the new sounds rocked by

Run-DMC (and to the new old sounds of the Chantels). Unfortunately, there was also a meat-headed minority who insisted on demonstrating their fear of music they'd never before heard—the crew performed "It's Like That," "30 Days," and "Rock Box"—by running up and down the aisles of the theater booing at the top of their lungs while Run-DMC were onstage.

Mostly, however, Run-DMC, and rap in general, were doing very well by the summer of 1984. And down in Orlando, Florida, a smart 31-year-old black concert promoter named Ricky Walker couldn't help but notice. He'd worked as the Commodores' production manager throughout the Seventies, was the national promotions director for the Jacksons World Tour in 1979, and had run the Kool Jazz Fest in Orlando and in Atlanta, his home base, for several years. Ricky had also been trying for a while to put together a "concept" show pitched to younger ticket buyers. His original idea along these lines was "The Great American Funk-Out," starring Rick James, Prince, Lakeside, the Barkays, Cameo, and the Gap Band. But one day in Orlando while he was promoting the Kool Jazz Fest, he suddenly grasped that rap, not funk, was the music of choice for younger music lovers.

When Ricky flew to New York, the cradle of rap, to sign up the talent he needed, his first stop was Sylvia Robinson at the Sugarhill Records recording studio-and-office complex in Englewood, N.J. Unfortunately, the promoter from down South and the Queen of Rap could not reach an agreement. Undaunted, Ricky stopped next at Rush Productions in the hope that Russell Simmons might allow Run-DMC to join his event, which he was now calling the New York City Fresh

Festival. Russell had a better idea: Rush Productions would provide the Fresh Feat with all the rap talent it needed.

Russell's Rush Productions offices then occupied a little two-room suite on the ninth floor of a funky old office building at 1133 Broadway, just south of 26th Street in Manhattan. It was hardly a fashionable location. The record business in New York is pretty much centered along the power alley that is 57th Street, as are the rest of the major entertainment corporations. Thirty blocks down Broadway there is no big business. It is a neighborhood of discount third-world imports: cameras and audio equipment, clothes, sporting goods, rugs, toys, and furnishings. Indians, Chinese, Japanese, Arabs, and Africans move through the streets, and certain blocks are fragrant with the smell of curry.

Russ started at 1133 with one desk in the offices of Prep/Street Records—J.B. Moore and Robert Ford, proprietors—in August of 1981. When J.B. and Rocky closed up shop a year later, Russell stayed in the building, renting a tiny one-room office on the fourth floor. He also inherited Rocky and J.B.'s entire staff in the person of 19-year-old Heidi M. Smith. Heidi had been the brightest of Rocky's students at the Institute of New Cinema Artists' Recording Industry Training Program, his intern while she was still a highschooler, and his assistant once she graduated. Heidi was the whole of Russ's fulltime staff when Ricky Walker came calling early in the summer of 1984. By that time, Russ was managing not only Run-DMC and Kurtis Blow, but rappers Whodini, Dr. Jeckyll & Mr. Hyde, Jimmy Spicer, Spyder D and Sparky D, and singer Alyson Williams. He and Ricky decided that Kurt and Whodini would join the Fresh Fest with Run-DMC, and that it would be a good idea to invite the Fat Boys, too, a trio from Brooklyn whose hit records were then being produced by Kurtis Blow.

Whodini was also a Brooklyn trio, but there their similarities to the Fat Boys, or to any other rap act, end. Comprised of the rappers Jalil Hutchins and John "Ecstacy" Fletcher and deejay Grandmaster D (born Drew Carter), the good-looking members of Whodini justifiably billed themselves as "the sex symbols of rap." They were signed to Jive Records, a label whose parent company was in England, and they recorded in London. By the summer of '84 they'd racked up a pair of bona fide radio hits: "Magic's Wand," a tribute to pioneering WBLS rap deejay Mr. Magic, and "The Haunted House of Rock."

Whodini had also just finished recording their second album, a Larry Smith production entitled *Escape*, which would give birth to several big hits: "Five Minutes of Funk," "Friends," and "Freaks Come Out at Night." These smashes powered Whodini's show on the road—along with the dancers Dr. Ice and the Kangol Kid (on loan from UTFO, who'd step out on their own on the strength of "Roxanne Roxanne" a few months later), Ecstacy's leather shorts and go-go boots, and the great Grandmaster D's crowd-pleasing ability to scratch up "Good Times" with his mouth.

Ricky also signed up the breakdancing crews Magnificent Force, Uptown Express, and the Dynamic Breakers to provide between-rappers entertainment on a second stage. The whole show was designed to move along very quickly and professionally (eight acts in three hours), and boasted such amenities as state-of-the-art lights and sound, and meticulous advance promotion. The natty young businessman had even boiled down his philosophy into a rap-ish rhyme with a distinctly Southern flavor: "If you got something to sell, you can't yell it in a well. You got to stand up in the trees and raise a lot of hell." If everything went as planned, the Fresh Fest, aimed at 10,000 to 20,000-seat arenas from coast to coast, would bring rap to a whole new audience.

But first he had to make believers out of the doubters. For all of Ricky's enthusiasm and experience, when he began talking to venue operators about a national rappers and breakers tour, he went over like Columbus addressing a meeting of the Flat Earth Society. Skepticism was so high that a salesman at a radio station in Greensboro, North Carolina—whose Coliseum, over the Labor Day weekend, was to be the site of the first test date—initially declined to take Ricky's money.

"You're a friend of mine," the salesman said. "Can't I talk you out of doing this show?"

Ricky laughed last. The show sold 7400 tickets in four hours, and soon sold out all 9000 seats. The second test date, at Atlanta's seat Omni, also sold out. The conclusion—especially now that Swatch Watch had come aboard as the Fresh Fest's sponsor, was unavoidable: "On with the show!"

And it really was a great show, on a par with the Motown Revues of the mid-Sixties, when for $3 you could see Stevie Wonder, Mary Wells, Marvin Gaye, the Temptations, Smokey Robinson & the Miracles, the Marvelettes, Martha & the Vandellas, and Kim Weston. Now, twenty years later, a fiendish hiphop head could catch a comparable bunch of vital young hitmakers for $10—and they *all* had hits that fall. Run-DMC, at the top of the bill, played a set that included "It's Like That," "Sucker MCs," "Hard Times," "Jam Master Jay," "Rock Box," "30 Days" and "Hollis Crew." Kurt was hitting with "8 Million Stories" and "AJ Scratch," a salute not only to the great DJ AJ (Aaron O'Bryant), but to the everloving Bronx—"where the people are fresh." Whodini's three "F" records ("Friends," "Freaks," and "Funk") would all end up in the Black Singles Top 5. The Fat Boys had "Fat Boys," "Can You Feel It," "Don't You Dog Me," and "Jailhouse Rap." And Newcleus, a nine-person troupe from Brooklyn's Bedford-Stuyvesant neighborhood led by Benjy "Cosmo D" Cenac in his bowler hat, had a Top Ten Black single with "Jam On It," a catchy little novelty that featured rappers whose voices had been speeded up, which lent the song that comical old Chipmunks effect.

Run's show throughout the tour was essentially the same as it had been for a while, with this exception: When Run himself finally hit the stage, all music would cease. "Y'all seen a whole bunch of great acts out here tonight," he'd announce, "But I want y'all to know one goddamn thing." Pausing dramatically, until he was sure that all ten thousand party people were listening, he'd then shout, *"This is my motherfucking house!"* It was an outrageous boast, and one that usually set the whole place howling, which energy Run would rev up even further by leading the crowd in a little question-and-answer routine. "*Whose* house?" he'd wonder and cup his ear. "*Run's* house!" came the thunderous reply. He'd ask the same question and get the same answer several times, setting up a rhythm, and finally Jay would cut in the beat to "Hard Times" or "It's Like That" and it was all over—it *was* Run's house.

Backstage Run proved his mettle the hard way, in head-to-head battles with the other rappers. On at least one occasion it was Run versus Jalil and Kurtis in a rapid-fire exchange of rhymed insults. Jalil and Kurt ganged up on Run:

first 'Lil would make up a rhyme about Run, and Run would bat it back with a rhyme of his own about Jalil, then Kurt would attack Run, and Run would have to come right back and kick Kurt's butt. So here was Run making up twice as many rhymes as his competitors—and winning, too. After three or four innings, both 'Lil and Kurt were literally rolling on the floor laughing at Run's def disses, unable to defend themselves any longer.

Run-DMC were also having to face more public challenges as well. D remembers coming back into town after having been out on the road for four straight days, and running into an old pal who congratulated him on the crew's new record. At the time Run-DMC didn't *have* a new record. What this friend was talking about was a jam by a Brooklyn crew named Divine Sounds who were hitting with "What People Do for Money," which sounded a *lot* like "It's Like That."

When D first heard it he got real mad and thought, "People bitin' us!" Later that night he was pleased to discover that he wasn't the only one who recognized the theft. He was at home listening to "Mr. Bill" Stephney over radio station WBAU, out of Adelphi University. Bill would shortly sign on to become national director of promotions for Def Jam Recordings and a charter member of the Bomb Squad, Public Enemy's production team. But then he just happened to be a real smart radio deejay. He spun "What People Do for Money" and cut it up with "It's Like That." The tune's styles and tempo are *very* similar, and Mr. Bill was able to get across his amusing point without saying a word: what Divine Sounds had done for money was bite Run-DMC's record. D thought it was funny, too, but underneath it all he was a little worried that these imitators might end up stealing Run-DMC's style for *good*.

Back on the road, the 1984 Swatch Watch New York City Fresh Fest concluded a solid run of nearly four months with several shows in Hawaii at Christmastime. The tour had been a smash, with the bottom-line spelled out in an *Amusement Business* headline at the end of the year: SWATCH WATCH TOUR GROSSES $3.5 MILLION IN 27 PERFORMANCES.

But the Fresh Fest was more than a moneymaker; it was a ground-breaker. It played in cities where *no* rap was played on the radio, like Chicago, and still sold ten thousand seats. In cities where they loved rap, like Philadelphia, the tour sold out the 19,000-seat Spectrum, quickly added a show, and sold another ten thousand seats in one day. And in markets like Providence, which is hardly a chocolate city, a full thirty-five percent of the nine thousand tickets sold at the Providence Civic Center were bought by whites. In sum, said Ricky Walker proudly, "The first Fresh Fest was like the pioneering of rock'n'roll all over again, just like those barnstorming Alan Freed tours of the Fifties."

And he was right.

FIVE

Def Jam

In the spring of 1984, when Run-DMC had been on the road more or less constantly for a year, a very influential 12-inch rap single was released in New York City on the independent Party Time label. The artists were T. LaRock and Jazzy Jay, the name of the jam was "It's Yours," the producer was someone named Rick Rubin, and it was an instant b-boy smash. Everything about the record seemed new and fresh and exciting. T. LaRock, to begin with, was a hell of rapper and, apparently, an even better writer. The vocabulary of the lyrics was very advanced. Even the introduction was a showstopper, a deep-voiced rapper inviting the entire universe to join him in some fun: "Commentating, illustrating, description-giving, adjective experts, analyzing, summarizing musical myth-seeking, People of the Universe—This is yours!"

But it was the beat, of course, that was the prime attraction for b-boys. The arrangement was very spare, much like

"Sucker MCs," but somehow—maybe because it had a more conventional verse-chorus-verse structure—it seemed even more dynamic. It was the debut on wax of all concerned. T. LaRock, born Terry Keaton, was the solo-rapping younger brother of Special K of the Treacherous Three (who actually wrote most of the lyrics to "It's Yours"). DJ Jazzy Jay, from the Bronx like T, was an original member of rapper Afrika Bambaataa's Zulu Nation, and had toured with Bam's Soul Sonic Force following the international success of the group's aptly-named "Planet Rock" in 1982.

But there likely would have been no record if not for Rick Rubin. At the time, Rubin was a 21-year-old music-loving student at New York University. A film and video production major, he also played in a band called Hose, which was, he remembers, "like Black Sabbath but a little more psychedelic." Actually, they were probably *considerably* more psychedelic, given that their repertoire consisted not only of originals but of heavy-metal cover versions of funk anthems like Hot Chocolate's "You Sexy Thing," the Ohio Players' "Fire," and Rick James' "Super Freak."

Rick's affection for black music, and for rap in particular, stretched back to his high-school days in Long Beach, Long Island. He recalled the town as "wealthy, mostly Jewish, with some Italians. The east end of Long Beach is upper-middle-class Jewish and Italian. Center of town is a black ghetto. The west end is a white ghetto, mostly Irish with some Italians . . . and all the kids went to the same high school, mine. Long Beach City High School was about seventy percent white and thirty percent black and it used to close because of race riots."

A fan even then of extreme rock'n'roll, Rick had played for a while in a "hardcore" band called The Pricks. Hardcore is a very fast, loud, angry and basic kind of rock that had been pioneered in the early Eighties in southern California by groups like Black Flag and X. It is exciting and powerful music, but it has never caught on in a big way. This failure created a turning point in Rick's life. "If the white kids had liked hardcore, I would never have gotten involved in rap music. But the fact that new music is stifled, instead of embraced, by white teens, is what forced me to like rap music," he recalls. "It was exciting and happening. There was a scene building, and there wasn't a scene building in hardcore. Nobody cared."

Expanding on this theme, Rick noted, "I don't know why white kids are content to listen to the same old stuff year after year without experimenting and looking for something a bit different and fresh, but unfortunately that would seem to be the case. The white kids at my high school liked the Stones, Sabbath, the Who or Zeppelin—groups that were either dead or might as well have been. They were easy to like, but rarely toured, so there was no energy you could be involved with.

"It turned out that the black kids in my school were into music I found much more exciting and accessible. They were always waiting for the new rap records to come out. It was so exciting that people could be so progressive musically that they'd want the newest thing, love it, and it would make them forget everything else."

It was his affection and admiration for the music of Run-DMC, Rick says, that inspired him to produce "It's Yours." At the time he had no experience at all as a producer, but went ahead anyway, reasoning, "There is no real way to learn how to produce; you just have to do it. Jazzy and T. LaRock didn't come to me; I went to them. I knew they have never made a record before and wanted to. I thought I knew how to do it and did." Simple.

Rick and Russ met for the first time at Danceteria in the spring of 1984, a few weeks after the release of "It's Yours." Danceteria was then one of the truly hip rock clubs in the city, presenting different kinds of music on each of several floors every night, and consequently attracting a very mixed crowd. Introduced to Russ as "Rick who did 'It's Yours,'" Rick Rubin made a very strong and favorable impression on Russ. "I couldn't believe it," Russ remembers. "He liked all the same records I did, and they weren't all selling. He understood the music better than most of the people making it."

Rick recalls that "we found that we both liked and disliked the same things in music, except that we came to it from different directions. Russell like beat-oriented material derived from r&b, and I liked beat-oriented material based in rock, like AC/DC and Aerosmith. In both cases, it was dance music that was a reaction against boring disco." This question of beats is crucial. "What differentiates our records from disco records is the kick drum," Rick says. "Rock goes: boom ba-*cha*, boom-boom ba-*cha*. The pulse beat of disco goes: *boom boom boom boom boom*." In other words, rap and rock favor heavy accents on the second and fourth beats of a measure, while disco favors four even accents per measure.

Rick and Russ met at the Rush Productions office and immediately started conspiring. "I asked Russell if there was anything he could do to promote the T. LaRock record around the country," Rick said. "He told me how it all worked, but I was concerned that he'd made maybe twenty records that I thought were tremendous and he wasn't wealthy.

"I never got paid on the T. LaRock record, and Russ told me a lot of hard stories about all the records that he'd never got paid for, so I knew that if both of us were to continue to make records, we'd have to do it ourselves. That way we could promote our groups the way we wanted to, and use the money we made to make them bigger —which labels that are only interested in fast money won't do."

It was almost no sooner said than done. Rick and Russ each kicked in $4000. Then they hooked up a manufacturing and distribution system, and by November 1984 they were rolling. "The purpose of this company," Russell told *Billboard*, "is to educate people to the real value of real street music by putting out records nobody in the business would distribute but us."

As good as their word, the first Def Jam twelve-inch was "I Need a Beat" by LL Cool J. Released in November, it cost $700 to produce and quickly went on to sell over 100,000 copies. LL was a sixteen-year-old phenomenon out of St. Albans in Queens, a neighborhood adjoining Hollis, who'd been rapping since the age of nine, and who felt he was ready for the big time. He'd sent off a self-produced basement demo tape to dozens of the companies, large and small, who were making rap records—including one to Rick Rubin, who'd produced "It's Yours." Rick was the only label exec who responded. The tape reached him in Room 802 of Weinstein Hall at NYU, which doubled as the offices of Def Jam and as Rick's dorm room. *Rockamerica* magazine, in a June 1985 piece, captured the ambience there pretty well: "a swirl of twelve-inch records, dirty t-shirts, tennis shoes, numerous turntables in various states of disrepair. . . . " There was also a huge Trouble Funk poster on the wall, a stack of hard-core porn and wrestling magazines, and an unmade bed.

English journalist Paolo Hewitt, who visited Rick in his room for *New Musical Express* in March 1985, recalls listening to records with the young producer: "He cranks the volume to an almost unbearable level, sits in his chair and, with eyes tightly closed, concentrates on every sound and every detail with an almost manic intensity. When the tune finishes Rick remains transfixed in this position for about ten seconds and then . . . boom! . . . he'll snap out of it, smile, and change the record." It was to Weinstein that Rick invited LL. "He was pretty good," Rick remembers. "So he wrote the lyrics, I wrote the music, and we put them together."

This casual story illustrates Russ's contention that Rick "is just about the best goddamn A&R man [talent scout] I have ever seen. If he gets a sniff, hears a *word*, he's on to it. And he can feel what is right for the kids. He *knows* the music." Russell backed up his belief in the sureness of Rick's golden ear by having Rush take on the management of the Def Jam acts.

Rick's opinion, at least with regard to LL, was seconded by Russell's younger brother. As soon as he heard "I Need a Beat," Run told anyone who'd listen that LL was "the best ever." They battled once at the Rush offices and it was titanic, lasting 20 minutes easily, with the two of them snapping on each other at twice the speed of the battle Run had had with Jalil and Kurt. That is, Run would say the first line of his rhyme—and LL would finish it, and turn it against Run in the process! They battled at the top of their voices, chasing each other from one room to the other (by this time Rush had expanded to two rooms), out into the hall, and then back in again. When it was all over, Run was asked who'd started the fight. "I did!" he snapped. "I don't like that man!" A couple of months later, backstage at Madison Square Garden for a benefit basketball game against WRKS, New York, it was time for a group shot of all the celebrity ballplayers. Run stood by LL, saying, "Let me get over here next to my son."

Clearly L was an original, a very macho hardcore rapper with undeniable sex appeal and, more particularly —given his dimples and his overall good looks—with *teen* sex appeal not unlike that of New Edition.

Indeed, LL was not above writing rap love songs. He first expressed his more romantic feelings on "I Want You," the a-side of his very next single, which captures the particulars of puppy love as well as it's ever been done: "I tell you that my sister isn't here today/You go away but I wish you'd stay/Girl, I'm twisted around your finger/When you leave your perfume lingers/I want you."

This young man, born James Todd Smith, also had a clear understanding of the outlaw nature of rap, as demonstrated in a rhyme from "I Need a Beat"—"I'm in the center of a musical scorcher. To some citizens it's a form of torture/They hear me, they fear me, my funky poetry, I'm improving the conditions of the rap industry."

In December 1984 Def Jam unleashed an even more unlikely act on the rap world—the Beastie Boys. The Beasties were three young white kids who'd started out in hardcore bands in 1979 when they were still in junior high school. Comprised of Adam Yauch, Michael Diamond and some friends, they released a seven-inch EP entitled "Polly Wog Stew" on Rat Cage Records in January 1982. It contained eight songs (hardcore is *fast*), including such ditties as "Egg Raid on Mojo" and "Transit Cop."

The record won some good reviews, and the Beasties added Adam Horovitz on guitar. Horovitz had been in a band called the Young and the Useless, and is the son of the notable American playwright Israel Horovitz.

In August 1983 the band cut "Cookie Puss" backed with "Beastie Revolution" for Rat Cage. Formally, it is a smirkish quasi-rap record in which a young prankster phones up a real-life ice cream parlor in an attempt to talk to Cookie Puss, which he pretends to think is a person and not an ice cream cake fashioned in the shape of a cartoon character. The Beasties discovered that they couldn't easily reproduce "Cookie Puss" in concert, so in October 1983 they added to their lineup "DJ Double R"—also known as Rick Rubin—to scratch up the record onstage.

And more and more the Beasties turned to rap. As New York City kids, they'd followed and loved rap from the moment it surfaced on record, began to add some to their live shows, and discovered that that was the part that people liked best. By the summer of 1984 they were all rap, and in December Def Jam released "Rock Hard"/"The Party's Getting Rough"/"Beastie Groove." Like Rick, the Beasties favored a rap/hard rock mixture, a mix that certainly defines "Rock Hard," which finds the threesome rapping over the motivating riff from AC/DC's "Back in Black."

The next Def Jam release was a novelty record by Jazzy Jay. The a-side is a very funky little cut-and-scratch instrumental called "Def Jam," kicked off by Jazzy's Vocoderized announcement: "It's def . . . It's def . . . So def so def so def it's a def jam!" But it's the b-side, a track entitled "Cold Chillin' In the Spot," that is an overlooked treasure—the rapping debut of Russell Simmons himself. Actually, it's stretching it to say that Russ is *rapping*, but he is talking a lot of trash, sounding slightly drunk and very soulful in a style that recalls no one so much as . . . Eddie Cheba. After confessing, "I ain't never sung before. I'm a manager," and pointing out that Dr. Jeckyll's in the house and Jazzy Jay is in the place, Russ commences to dole out instructions to the listening and dancing audience: "People in the middle, y'all lift up your legs—both legs with both hands—and wiggle 'em in the air like this. You see me doing this? Can you do it? You lyin'! Y'all all lyin'!" Next Russ sees a pretty girl in the studio and starts coming on to her directly. "I got about two more minutes. When the two minutes is up, me and you is gonna shoot to the hotel and do the wildest thing!" Finally, he informs Dr. Jeckyll that the good doctor can't rap on this record—and neither can Run-DMC, Whodini, Kurtis Blow, LL Cool J or any of the other artists he manages—because those artists' record companies would sue him. "So," he says with a laugh. "I'll do the rap myself and keep *all* the money! Me and Rick gonna keep—Look at Rick laughin'!—gonna keep all the money. Let's go!" And the record's over.

The fourth Def Jam release matches up the Beastie Boys' MCA with a recording engineer friend of his named Burzootie (Jay Burnett) on a record called "Drum Machine."

The sixth release was Jimmy Spicer's "Beat the Clock." And Def Jam 007, released in the summer of 1985, was the Hollis Crew's "It's the Beat." Produced by Run-DMC, and featuring the tough rapping of their old pals Butter Love and Cool Tee, "It's the Beat" is a tribute to what is, in the Crew's opinion, the most important part of a song. . . .

> The force that invades every musical tone
> It sounds so def when the beat's alone
> It's not the funky fresh rhymes or the cuts galore
> It's the beat! Word! And that's for sure!

The Def Jam records really were def jams, but as Russ pointed out, "the best rap music is probably the most offensive to adults, especially black adults," which meant among other things that Def Jam had a rough time getting its records played on black radio—the chief promotional medium for the sale of records—which is *run* by black adults. The label succeeded anyway, according to Rick, because its records were "in tune with what's popular on the street," which translated into club play, in-store play, college radio play, highly positive reviews from the critics, and red-hot word-of-mouth. Also, as Russ pointed out, "a lot of the time our records *force* themselves onto the radio. Several program directors have told me that they personally hated 'I Need a Beat,' but after airing it twice, they couldn't keep it off their playlist because the phones jumped off the hook"—meaning that kids phoned in requests for it over and over again.

"The funniest thing is that rap is just black teenage music, the same black teenage music that the Jackson 5 made in 1970, and the same black teenage music that New Edition is making today. So I don't understand why New Edition can play on black radio and not LL Cool J. One is bubble gum and the other attracts a slightly older crowd —and the older one is 'I Need a Beat.' Believe me, you don't hear 'Mr. Telephone Man' in the clubs. You hear LL Cool J."

Things got considerably easier for Def Jam when they signed a distribution deal with Columbia Records, the largest record company in the world, in the fall of 1985. With Columbia behind them, Rick, then 22 years old, and Russ, 27, were able to take the time and spend the money necessary to make a whole album on LL. Entitled *Radio*, it quickly went gold, signifying sales of over half a million copies. They've gone on to make a double-platinum success out of the

Beasties' first album, *Licensed to Ill*, and to score major hits with Oran "Juice" Jones, Chuck Stanley, and Public Enemy.

The secret of Def Jam's success? "We do what we like," says Russell simply. "We're not trying to push anything on anybody: 'It's got a feeling. It's good. I like it. It's probably gonna sell.' That's how we make all our records."

Def Jam's success has not only made stars of the artists on its roster, it has made stars, at least within the record industry, of the two young men who founded the label. In fact, these days Russ and Rick look damn near like prophets. Early in 1985, *before* the hook-up with Columbia, Rick boasted: "The future of rap music is quite simply me and Def Jam, Rush Productions, all the artists on our roster. *That* is the future of rap music."

Run-DMC as twelve-year-olds: (top to bottom) Joseph Simmons, Darryl McDaniels, Jason Mizell.

Above: DMC, Russell Simmons, and Jam Master Jay with Steve
Plotnicki and Cory Robbins of Profile Records, circa 1984.
(Photo © by David Salidor.)

Below: Run-DMC with Larry Smith, March 1984.
(Photo © by Gene Bagnato.)

he Hollis Crew in Hollis, Queens, New York, October 1984. Runny Ray stands
ext to DMC, Cool T and Butter Love crouch in front. Fat Fluud, Jeff's brother,
: in the middle of the back row.
Photo © by Janette Beckman, 1985.)

Above: With Russell at the Rush Productions offices on lower Broadway, April 1985. (Photo © by James Hamilton.)

Below: LL Cool J and Run at Chung King Studios, Winter 1986. (Photo © by Claude "Paradise" Gray.)

Above: Recording "King Holiday" with Kurtis Blow (second from left) and Dexter King (second from right), fall 1985.
(Photo © by Talib Abdul Haqq, Wadcva Images.)

Below: Run-DMC versus apartheid, Columbia University, April 1985.
(Photo © by Chase Roe.)

Above: Backstage with Lou Reed and Jim Carroll at the taping of MTV's "Rock Influences" special, Capitol Theater, Passaic, New Jersey, September 25, 1984. (Photo © by Talib Abdul Haqq, Wadeva Images)

Below: Chillin' hard with Dick Clark on the set of "American Bandstand," August 1985. (Photo © by Glen E. Friedman.)

Above: Recording "Walk This Way" with Aerosmith, March 1986. Front row: Steve Tyler, JMJ, Rick Rubin, Joe Perry. Back row: DMC, Run, Russell, Bill Adler. (Photo © 1986 Lloyd Nelson.)

Below: On the set of "Tougher Than Leather" with director Rick Rubin, November 1986. (Photo © by Sebastian Piras.)

Above: Run with the Beastie Boys on the road with the Raising Hell Tour, July 1986. (Photo © by Ricky Powell.)

Below: Run-DMC with Barry White during KDAY's "Day of Peace", 1986

Rap group Run-D.M.C. and singer Barry White, second from right, call for one-day truce by L.A. gangs at press conference. Singers will host radio show on KDAY today.

Run-D.M.C. asks gangs for 'day of peace'

With Japanese b-boys in Tokyo on the last leg of the Raising Hell Tour, December 1986. (Photo © by Sadao Osada.)

With Lyor Cohen at the premiere of "Tougher Than Leather," New York City, September 1988. (Photo © by Ricky Powell.)

SIX

Kings of Rock

At the beginning of every week during the fall of 1984, when they were back in New York between Fresh Fest gigs, Run-DMC worked on their second album. *King of Rock* would hit the streets on January 15, 1985, less than ten months after the release of *Run-DMC*, which meant, among other things, that once again Russ and Larry had to do most of the production work themselves.

The difference this time was that Russ and Larry weren't getting along as well as they had during the making of the first album. "Our relationship started deteriorating on *King of Rock*," says Larry. "Rick started getting involved, so it was time for me to exit." In fact, Larry stayed on until the album was complete, but Rick made his influence felt in small ways: LL contributed the lyrics to "Can You Rock It Like This," and Rick himself rerecorded the guitar part, originally cut by Davy D, for the single version of "Jam Master Jammin'."

The basic rift, though, was between the group and Russell

on one side—who wanted to keep the music hard and rocking—and Larry, who wanted to move in a more "musical" direction and who wasn't as wild about rock. This tension resulted in the weakest of Run-DMC's first three albums. Many of the songs are individually strong, but the album as a whole simply isn't as unified as the other two. As Russell put it shortly after the completion of the album, "Run-DMC have done a couple of things to soften up. I didn't want them to go in that direction, so I think we'll be going to go back to our old format. The next one will be louder and meaner."

King of Rock picks up where *Run-DMC* leaves off—with a deejay's showcase. On *Run-DMC* the last cut on the second side is "Jay's Game." On *King of Rock* the first cut on the first side is "Rock the House." "Rock the House" keeps the listener off-balance by jaggedly slicing up several of the album's songs. As the track fades, we hear Run in the studio saying, "Run it back." An instant later, DMC is booming out the opening rhyme on "King of Rock," unquestionably the best song on the album, and one of the greatest of their career. Propelled by nothing more than a bomb-like kick drum, D brags:

> I'm the king of *rock*! There is none *higher*!
> Sucker emcees should call me *sire*!
> To burn my kingdom you must use *fire*!
> I won't stop rockin' till I *retire*!

In the next breath we're pummeled by a brand-new monster-rock guitar riff from Eddie Martinez and a brand-new world-conquering rhyme from Run:

> Now we rock the party and come correct
> All cuts are on time and rhymes connect
> Got the right to vote and will elect

And other rappers can't stand us—but give us respect
They call us ill We're getting iller. There's no one chiller
It's not Michael Jackson and this is not *Thriller*
I'm one def rapper. I know I can hang
I'm Run from Run-DMC, like Kool from Kool & the
    Gang

This was the standout track on the album as far as the critics
were concerned. *Rolling Stone* summed up the general feeling:
" . . . It lets Run-DMC crunch and pop like some sort of
hip-hop Black Sabbath."

"Roots, Rap, Reggae," a rap-reggae hybrid on the first side,
is one of the album's most interesting tracks, even if it isn't
entirely successful. Many a rapper has family roots in the
Caribbean and many another feels a spiritual kinship with
Jamaica's rudeboys—the island variation of America's
b-boys—and the music they make. D and J had long been
reggae fanatics, and were particularly wild about that brand
of reggae known as dub, which is a very stripped-down, funky
style not unlike Run-DMC's style of rap. Yellowman was the
king of dub. An African-Caribbean albino (hence his name)
with wooly yellow hair and big thick glasses, Yellowman is a
fairly freaky-looking gent—although his taste in
color-coordinated running suits and black bowler hats
definitely smacks of familiar b-boy stylee. More importantly,
he can write and rap his butt off, which is why the crew sought
him out when they decided they wanted a real Jamaican
rapper with them on their reggae track. D still remembers a
rhyme from a song called "I Can't Take It" from an album
by Yellowman & Fathead called *Bad Boy Shankin'*—"Life
was a thing money couldn't buy/Rich man live, poor man
die/I can't take it. . . . "

As it turned out, Yellowman just happened to be touring the U.S. at the time, and Russ was able to get in touch with him and convince him to take the job. He showed up very late one night at Greene Street expecting Run and D to hand him some lyrics. When it turned out that they weren't even on the premises, he went up to the mike and winged it. Unfortunately, Profile's Cory Robbins didn't like Yellow's first pass, so the rude boy went back and cut something new. His final rhyme, though relatively generic, is funny and relaxed: "Five to five equal to ten/Everywhere I go I got a lot of girlfrien'/Music is sweet, music is nice/Yellow have about twenty-four wife."

Back in the control room Russ and Larry, who had cut Run and D's vocals at a different session, were so delighted that they just rolled around laughing. "It wasn't Run-DMC trying to fake a Jamaican accent," Larry recalls. "When Yellowman opened his mouth, we all got real happy 'cause it was the realest thing."

Fake accent or not, Run did write one dandy little rhyme for the track that works as a kind of front-line dispatch on the state of the crew's career and how he feels about it: "Now, party people, I'm so happy I don't know what to do, 'cause I'm the emcee with the rhymes and down with the crew/Rock from Africa to France and to Kalamazoo, and everywhere that I play I hear a yay not a boo."

Still all the technical tricks in the world can't make up for the fact that Run-DMC and Yellowman were never in the same studio at the same time, which is finally what's wrong with the track.

"Can You Rock It Like This" was written by LL Cool J, sixteen years old at the time. A bemused meditation on the price of celebrity, it *sounds* a lot more like LL than like Run: "I've got jetset women who offer me favors. My face is a thousand lipstick flavors." Then again, the following rhyme sounds like no one but Run: "I'm straining, not complaining for a casual life, something normal, nothing formal, three kids and a wife." "You're Blind" was written for the most part by Tony Rome. Tony was an ambitious young man working as a custodian at Columbia University when he first hooked up with Russell. He ran Rush's fan clubs for a while, and then worked as Whodini's road manager during the fall of 1985 and LL's during the summer of 1986. "You're Blind" is not only the one "message song" on *King of Rock*, it is, with its description of "tenement buildings and skyscrapers," distinctly Melle Mel-ish. Perhaps unsurprisingly, Tony, like Mel, is from the Bronx.

"Darryl and Joe" is built on Larry's swirling, circusy keyboards. Once again, Run and D report on the state of their success, and on how they keep their balance:

> Traveling 'round the world with my mind at ease. No Calvin Kleins, just wearing Lees
> Got credit in places I've never been 'cause the records I write are in the Top Ten
> The top of the chart is where I stay, but I also chill around the way
> In Hollis, Queens is where I stalk, on the streets with the beats is where I walk.

Shortly after they finished recording the album, Run-DMC got together with director Joe Butt's Maverick Productions to make the video to "King of Rock." Like the "Rock Box" video, "King of Rock" features a well-known comic in the role of sucker emcee, in this case Calvert

DeForest, who was playing Larry "Bud" Melman on network television's "Late Night with David Letterman." The video opens with Run and D jogging up the steps of a large building, only to get stopped at the door by a smirking little guard (Melman). "This is a *rock'n'roll* museum," he sneers. "You don't belong here." He starts to laugh in their faces, but big D quickly pushes past the old troll, bumrushing the show as he booms out the song's opening line, "I'm the king of rock. . . . "

Once in the museum Run and D move from exhibit to exhibit, dissing one rock immortal after another. They stomp on Michael Jackson's sequined glove, smash Elton John's rhinestone glasses, jam one of their Stetsons onto a plaster bust of the Beatles, and shake their heads "no" at television monitors running performance footage of Little Richard, Buddy Holly, and Jerry Lee Lewis. When they finally come upon a monitor showing "Rock Box," the rappers turn to the camera with big smiles and nod *"yes!"*

This great music video adds a more specific meaning to the following lines in the song: "Now we crash through walls, go through floors, bust through ceilings, and knock down doors." In other words, try and stop us if you want, try and keep us in that little box called rap, but there's nothing you can do to keep us from getting what we deserve—and that is the recognition that our music is on a par with the greatest that has ever been made.

The funny thing is that when the album came out, the critics, at least, didn't argue. *Rolling Stone* said, "These guys are no mere pretenders to the throne." The *Los Angeles Times* advised its readers: "In Texas there's a saying—'If you're as good as you say you are, it ain't braggin'.' Run-DMC ain't braggin'." Similarly, the *Washington Post's* J.D. Considine noted: "Even their most outrageous rhymes are delivered with such undeniable flair that it's hard not to take them at face value."

The public dug the single, too. "King of Rock" went to number 19 on the Black Singles chart, three positions higher than its father, "Rock Box." What Run-DMC was attempting here was a delicate operation—how to expand their audience by attracting white rockers without alienating their core audience of black teens. In Russell's opinion, the crew was getting away with it "because what they do still sounds real. It's like the way James Brown used to cross over based on his real thing. I'm pleased we still get our records played in the Bronx."

Indeed, not only were Run-DMC still winning in the Bronx, MTV was playing the hell out of their new video, the critics were loving them, and the rock clubs were playing them. And suddenly England wanted a look at the group in the flesh. They flew to London for the first time on March 1, 1985 and spent the next ten days in England shaking hands and doing interviews. They also played four shows, one in Manchester, one in Nottingham, two in London. Apparently, they made a lot of friends. *Blues & Soul's* Ben Metcalfe raved about one of the London shows: "Throughout their all too brief set they never failed to impress with their incredibly tight delivery and commanding stage presence, whilst down on the turntables, Jam Master Jay didn't miss a beat. Nice work if you can get it!" Offstage, the crew had some trouble adjusting to a foreign culture, and particularly to English food. "Everything tasted real funny. The bacon had bones in it," recalls Run. "I just didn't see no future out there—but I was young and I didn't know no better."

Three days after they'd returned to the States, the crew had to hustle over to the Imperial Ballroom of midtown Manhattan's Sheraton Hotel to pick up an award from the New York Market Radio Broadcasters Association for a "VD rap" they'd recorded the previous year as a public service announcement for the New York State Health Department. It was a little 30-second spot entitled "Check It Out," recorded over a stark beat, but it won out over expensive productions by giants like the J. Walter Thompson Agency for the American Red Cross and Young and Rubicam for the U.S. Postal Service. The rhyme was simple and funny and effective:

> The other day I got the word from my girlfriend Sue
> She said, "I've got VD and you might have it, too."
> I said, "No way, no how, if I had it, I'd know it."
> She said, "That's not always true 'cause some people don't
>   show it."
> I said, "Where can I go to find out if I've got it?"
> "You can get help free from the Health Department."
> [Spoken] Yes, if you're told you might have VD, the state
>   health department says: Check it out!

In April 1985 Run-DMC was enlisted in another sort of battle, the fight against South African apartheid that was then being supported by students on many of the America's campuses. Despite the United Nations-sponsored international sports and cultural boycott of South Africa, the Reagan administration still maintained diplomatic and business ties with the country. Likewise, many of America's universities (which are businesses, too) had maintained their investments in American companies doing business in South Africa.

Many college kids across the country found it morally repulsive to attend institutions that made money off of a system that treated its black majority like slaves. They organized continuing protests to pressure their universities to take their money out of South Africa.

On April 15, 1985 the students at Columbia University—which is located in New York up near Harlem—were in the twelfth day of a strike protesting Columbia's investments in South Africa. Some students were camped out on the steps of a building called Hamilton Hall, which they had renamed Mandela Hall, in honor of Nelson Mandela, the South African freedom fighter who's been kept in jail by his government for over 20 years. Though it had been drizzling for hours, the students' spirits were high—and they were lifted much higher when Run-DMC (along with the Cold Crush Brothers from the Bronx) dropped by to perform for them toward the end of the afternoon.

DMC and Jay had come straight from airport and a gig in the midwest to bust out "Hard Times" and "It's Like That" for the strikers huddled under the tarp keeping off the rain. Run's pressing family commitments prevented him from making the show, so Jay took Run's place at the mike, with DJ Cut Creator, from LL Cool J's crew, handling the deejay chores. The Cold Crush Brothers, one of the great early rap groups, performed "Punk Rock Rap" and "Fresh, Fly, Wild and Bold," their two most recent records.

Jay did the gig on crutches. He had made the mistake the day before of following the example of road manager Runny Ray, who'd jumped out of a second-story motel room window in an effort to entertain himself. Ray, who probably landed on his head, was uninjured by the fall. Jay tried the same stunt and broke his leg. After the show, DMC told campus reporters that they'd performed that day because "We're against racism wherever it exists."

Two weeks later, the crew traveled to Princeton University in New Jersey to perform at a benefit for the students' Coalition for Divestment. The Coalition was in the middle of a semester-long struggle to convince the administration that it was wrong to have invested $330 million in companies doing business in South Africa. In March some 200 Princetonians had built a South African-styled "shantytown" in the middle of the McCosh courtyard, around which many of the college's classes are held. It stayed up through May.

The benefit's organizers included a pair of deejays from Princeton's radio station, Eric Weisbard and Sally Jacob, who'd been playing Run-DMC's records on the air. They reached out to the crew through Profile Records. "When Run-DMC heard about the cause, they wanted to play here," recalled Weisbard. "They're not the kind of band that *needs* to play at Princeton." Indeed, the crew deliberately asked the coalition not to announce the fact that they were appearing—although many of the 500 or so who showed up were not Princeton students, but kids from the surrounding community.

Run-DMC played on the afternoon of Sunday, April 28 on the campus's Cannon Green (so named for the Revolutionary War-era cannon that is its chief decoration), along with the Black Jacks, a Rolling Stones-styled band out of Boston, and the Love Pushers, a Top 40 group from Princeton. And thanks to the activism of those conscientious students—and their musical friends—Columbia and Princeton Universities began to divest.

Run- DMC devoted May of 1985 to the filming of the movie "Krush Groove." Their opportunity to make the film had opened up several months earlier with the publication of a story in the *Wall Street Journal*. On December 4, 1984 the newspaper of record for the international business community had run a front-page story about rap music. The writer was a young woman named Meg Cox, who had been contacted by Rocky Ford with the suggestion that she consider doing a story on this exciting—and moneymaking—new scene. Meg thought it was a good idea, researched and wrote the story, and even contributed a rhyming headline: "IF A BIG BEAT ZAPS YOU OUT OF A NAP, THE MUSIC IS RAP." But," continued the subhead: "If You Don't Clap or Tap or React, Maybe You're a Victim of a Culture Gap." The story noted that rap was "moving mainstream" and that "Mr. [Russell] Simmons, 26, now represents 17 acts and is known as the mogul of rap."

Israeli moviemaker Menahem Golan, reading the story on a flight between between New York and London, was thunderstruck by inspiration. His Cannon Films had already made "Breakin'" and "Breakin' 2," and he decided on the spot that his next movie would be called "Rappin'." As soon as he landed in London he called his New York office and barked, "Find me Russell Simmons!"

Russell had always wanted to make a movie about rap featuring his artists, but he wanted to do it *right*, in a way that was true to the scene as he knew it, and which was consistent with the images he'd been working with his artists to create. As badly as he wanted to make a movie, Russell would never get involved in something that was, in his words, "fake." The previous year he'd turned down no less a figure than Harry Belafonte, who'd wanted Russ and Rush to be a part of a movie Belafonte was shooting up in the South Bronx. Russ didn't like the sound of it and declined to participate. Belafonte went ahead anyway and made the movie that became "Beat Street," a story about the struggles of a graffiti artist, which featured performance cameos (and a sound track album) by Grandmaster Flash & the Furious Five, the Treacherous Three, and Afrika Bambaataa & the Soul Sonic Force plus Shango. Russell pronounced it "garbage." At about the same time, DMC recalled "driving past one of these movie houses and I saw this sign: BREAK DANCE AND RAP MUSIC. I just thought to myself, 'All that flick probably has is fake dance and crap music.'"

Golan was convinced that rap—like the short-lived breakdancing craze—would die out in a matter of weeks, and that the only way to squeeze any dough out of this latest teenaged spasm was to jump on it and rush out a rap quickie. He would have a script written in ten days, shoot the film the next month, and slot it into movie theaters in time for Easter vacation of 1985.

Predictably, Russell and Golan didn't hit it off. "I've been working for ten years to make this music mean something," Russell told Golan. "You can come in with one film and ruin everything I'm trying to build." Unperturbed, Golan shrugged and replied, "I am going to make this movie with you or without you, even if I have to go to Kansas to find the rappers I need."

As it turned out, Golan made "Rappin'" in Pittsburgh. It is the story of a rapping gangleader who's out to prove that he's a decent fellow even if he does rap and wear kettles on his head. Larry Smith signed on as the flick's music supervisor, a decision that deepened the rift between him and Russell. The only credible rapper involved with the movie was Lovebug Starski, who performed the title track, but who was never seen onscreen. It starred Mario Van Peebles, a very good-looking kid who clearly knew nothing about rap or the rap scene.

(Mario, incidentally, is the real-life son of Melvin Van Peebles, the writer, director, and star of one of Russell's favorite early seventies films, the notorious "Sweet Sweetback's Baadasssss Song," about a black man who kills a corrupt white cop and gets away with it. Melvin would have his own minor adventure in the rap world as the director of the "Funky Beat" music video for Whodini in the spring of 1986.)

But Golan wasn't the only show-businessman who read Meg Cox's story that day. Twenty-seven-year-old George Jackson also saw it. A native of Harlem and a graduate of Harvard—and of Fordham Prep in the Bronx before that—George was then working in Los Angeles for Richard Pryor's Orchid Productions. When the Fresh Festival came to the Long Beach Arena a few days after the *Journal*'s story, Jackson was in the house, along with his partners Doug McHenry and director Michael Schultz. Hollywood's preeminent black director, Schultz was very impressed with Run-DMC. "They had sold out 14,000 seats in Los Angeles on the same night, and in the same town, as the last date of the Jacksons' Victory Tour. I realized that this was a major group in the making, so as a filmmaker I had to stay up with what the kids were doing."

George was worried that Russ might end up making a deal with Golan, so he went to New York and ambushed Russell following one of Russ' meetings with the man from Cannon. George had described Russ to two of his larger friends and hired them to nab Russ as soon as he walked out of Golan's office. In the end both of these guys missed Russell, so it was up to the burly ex-football playing Jackson himself to make the play. Jackson claims that when the Russ hit the lobby he grabbed the young manager in a headlock, insisting that he sit down and talk with him immediately about making a movie with Jackson and his partners.

Russell was duly impressed by Jackson's enthusiasm and by the production team he'd assembled. Schultz was the director of "Cooley High," "Car Wash," and "Which Way Is Up" (the latter two featuring Richard Pryor), all of which Russell had loved. Schultz's most recent success had been Berry Gordy's "The Last Dragon." McHenry had worked as a production executive on "Thank God It's Friday" with Donna Summer, "Midnight Express," "Time Bandits," and "Foxes," and had produced music videos starring Cheryl Lynn, Midnight Star, and Shalamar.

The Los Angeles filmmakers' original idea was to make a concert documentary of the Fresh Festival show. Russell convinced them instead to make a full-length feature film starring his rappers, and then signed on as associate producer and co-executive producer of the sound track album. He felt a lot more comfortable knowing that he'd be working with these young black filmmakers than with the people at Cannon.

The movie's working title was "Rap Attack." Eventually, it would be called "Krush Groove." Schultz recalls that finding funding for it was "a major ordeal." "The decision makers in Hollywood are mostly WASP and Jewish, and they feel a lot safer dealing with the life-styles that they know—and they don't know black lifestyles or that audience," he said.

Eventually funding was found, and the producers hired

Ralph Farquhar to write the script. Farquhar, a young black man, had written scripts for such television shows as "Happy Days," "Laverne & Shirley," "Fame," and "The Odd Couple." Russell recalls that the first draft of Farquhar's script for "Krush Groove" was "as much about a white girl trying to break into the music business as it was about the New York rap scene." Given that Russell's original concept for the flick was to fictionalize the real-life story of June Bug—a popular Disco Fever deejay killed in a drug deal, and the young man to whose memory Run-DMC's first album was dedicated—Russell felt his first misgivings about the direction of the film. "But when they rewrote it, I still thought it could be great," he said. "It was the first film with all the real talent."

The final plot of "Krush Groove" is a kind of Hollywood-ization of the real-life story of Run-DMC, Russell Simmons, Rick Rubin and Def Jam Recordings. As in real life, a young record promoter named Russell (played by Blair Underwood) manages the career of his younger brother, a rapper named Run. As in real life, Russell is partners with a young white college kid named Rick, who runs their record company out of his room at a dormitory on a college campus.

Likewise, the subplot featuring the Fat Boys has a basis in real life. The three young rappers from Brooklyn's East New York had won their first record contract as the grand prize in a talent show, which is also what happens in the flick. And, as in the movie, they weren't called the Fat Boys at first—they were known as the Disco Three.

But all the business about Russell and Rick getting involved with gangster loan sharks is, as Run put it, "just Hollywood." And the only reason Prince protégé Shiela E appears in the movie is because the producers thought it needed some "love interest," and because she recorded for Warner Brothers Records, a sister company of Warner Brothers Films, the company distributing the film. The rappers thought that if there had to be a love interest (which is debatable), the part should have naturally gone to a good-looking female rapper like the Real Roxanne.

But the movie does star Run-DMC and Kurtis Blow as themselves, and it does feature cameo performances by LL Cool J, the Beastie Boys, Dr. Jeckyll & Mr. Hyde, and New York radio deejay Mr. Magic, as well as by popular non-rappers New Edition. It also features Russell himself as a club owner, and Run and Russell's father, Daniel Simmons, as their preacher father.

And then there's the handsome young Sidney Poitier-type named Blair Underwood, who plays "Russell Walker." At the time Blair was a 20-year-old who'd piled up some credits as a daytime soap opera player and an appearance or two on "The Cosby Show." He is a nice person and a pretty fair actor, but he is also a middle-class guy from Tacoma, Washington, who had no knowledge at all of the New York rap scene, nor any way of even faking it credibly—though he studied for his part by hanging out a lot with Russell. Bottom line: Blair was badly miscast.

It might have been much better to cast Fab Five Freddy in the role, as Russell had suggested. Freddy is the tall, good-looking, ultra-cool graffiti artist and downtown scenemaker mentioned by name in Blondie's "Rapture." It was also Freddy who played the promoter called Phade in the first rap movie, "Wild Style" (1983). In fact, Fred auditioned for "Krush Groove" but failed to thrill Schultz, so Blair got the part instead.

The movie was shot in Manhattan (at old faithful Danceteria) and the Bronx (at even older and more faithful Disco Fever) in 26 days in May of 1985 for a budget of about $3 million, which is not only fast, it's cheap—Schultz had had $10 million to lavish on "The Last Dragon." Though they had reservations about it later, the members of Run-DMC enjoyed making "Krush Groove." Filming proceeded quickly, with the rappers pausing only to translate into rap slang virtually every line of dialog Farquhar had written.

This dickering over dialogue was constant. "If it was up to Russell, he'd have someone saying 'motherfucker' every 20 seconds," Schultz recalled with a laugh. "Sometimes we'd end up with two sentences where nine-tenths of it was slang. I'd say, 'Look, let's put in a little English now and then, so the uninitiated will know what we're saying."

Russell wasn't laughing. "They think they have to water it down to cross it over, but in the process they lose authenticity, which is worth more than instant universal intelligibility," he said. "There is no substitute for authenticity." Ultimately, it was on the basis of its raw language that "Krush Groove" was rated "R" by the Motion Pictures Association of America.

Sheila E. told *Rock & Soul* that making the movie was "a great experience." "Not only did I get shown how to act," she said. "I was taught how to rap, too." That of course is a matter of debate. The scene in the movie in which Sheila raps generated derisive laughter and hisses in equal measure, at least in New York movie houses. During production she pretty much kept to herself, although she was visited on the set by Prince. Afterwards LL Cool J—who introduced his hit song "I Can't Live Without My Radio" in the movie—said, "Prince and his boys thought that we were making 'Shiela E.

Goes to Hollywood,' when the film was really about my homeboys Run and Kurtis Blow."

Run-DMC themselves had more specific criticisms. Jay thought the film was way offbase to have allowed Shiela E. to slap Run in the face. Run himself, who in the movie deserts his brother for another manager, said, "I'd never be disloyal to my brother. Russell is a good manager and producer, and a better brother hasn't been born yet. He knows what he's doing and I have a lot of respect for him." In a pretty bitter summation for *Rolling Stone*, Run said, "'Krush Groove' was nothing but a Walt Disney movie. The Fat Boys were just being funny, and I didn't do nothing."

The critics, too, expressed some pretty serious reservations about the movie when it debuted on October 25. Indeed, Janet Maslin of the *New York Times* could've been speaking for the rappers themselves when she wrote: "The skimpy screenplay insists upon entangling the performers in the most conventional subplots imaginable. . . . Rap music is infinitely more original than these creaky devices, and it deserves something better." Run's acting was singled out for praise by *Blitz*, an English magazine, which claimed that his "witty, diffident arrogance makes for the only really engaging character interest."

Notwithstanding the critics, "Krush Groove" was an immediate popular success. It opened in 515 theaters and grossed over $3 million in its first weekend—including over a million dollars in New York City alone—which made it the number one film in the country, according to the following week's *Variety*. And the soundtrack turned out to be an even bigger smash than the movie itself. Kurtis Blow hit with "If I Ruled the World," LL with "I Can't Live Without My Radio," Sheila E. with "Love Bizarre," the Beasties with "She's On It,"

Chaka Khan with "You Can't Stop the Street," and the Force MD's with "'Tender Love." Only Run-DMC themselves, who cut no new songs for the movie, had no hits in "Krush Groove."

Oddly, for all its innocence, "Krush Groove" touched off trouble at a few of the theaters at which it was playing in the New York area. "MOVIE SPARKS NEW TEEN RIOT, VICTIM   HURLED   INTO   WINDOW—200 STITCHES," screamed the *New York Post* on November 4. The *New York Times* more calmly noted that a 17-year-old youth from Franklin Square, Long Island had been thrown through a window following a local screening of "Krush Groove," and that two weekends earlier two people had been injured when a crowd of young fans charged the closed doors of a suburban theater showing the movie.

"'Krush Groove' does not appear to be a film likely to set off sparks," the *Times* murmured. "Unlike such other popular movies as 'Death Wish 3' and 'Rambo,' anger and revenge are not among its themes. Nor does it depict gang warfare as did 'The Warriors,' a film that was linked to violence at theaters a few years ago."

Time magazine's take was positively light-hearted. As part of their review of the movie, which was all in rhyme, the national newsweekly noted: "Now there've been fights at the Plexes, kids've got out of hand/But they must've spiked the sodas at the popcorn stand/Because this movie has the innocence of bygone years/Like the films of Fred ('Rock Around the Clock') F. Sears."

All kidding aside, the *Times* did speak to one Franklin Square resident with a reasonable explanation. "[The movie] is attracting a black crowd to a white town," noted a 15-year-old white youth. "That means trouble, especially because they come out of the movie all psyched up."

These incidents were the strange end to an unsatisfactory chapter in Run-DMC and Russell's career. "It was the first time I had to compromise something with my name on it as a producer, and I wasn't going to do any more of it," he said afterward. "I didn't like the producers telling me that Warner Brothers made them cut the film, so they had to cut it. They're suckers! If I get involved with the film business again, it's never going to be that way for me."

But it was Run who ended up taking most of the heat for the movie. An English journalist who insisted that the fight scene in "Krush Groove" qualified the entire movie as "violent," pushed the rapper past exasperation. "That film was a *cartoon!*" he yelled "Popeye beats up Bluto, but I bet you don't nag Popeye, do ya, sucker!"

SEVEN

When the People Gave and the Poor Got Paid

Run-DMC kicked off the summer of 1985 on May 31 as the headliners of the second annual Fresh Festival. It began scarcely five months after the end of the first Fresh Fest, and featured essentially the same lineup: Run at the top of the bill, Whodini, and the Fat Boys. This crew was filled out with West Coast breakdancers Shabba-Doo and Boogaloo Shrimp (the stars of the movies 'Breakin'' and 'Breakin' 2"), the Double Dutch Girls (a team of superb rope-jumpers who did their stuff to records by Prince), the Dynamic Breakers (back again from the first Fresh Fest), 17-year-old Chad (who hoped he'd be mistaken for the young Michael Jackson), and 12-year-old Jermaine Dupri, a talented young moonwalker who just happened to be the son of Mike Mauldin, the tour's production manager.

Kurtis Blow started out on the tour, but quickly withdrew

when he discovered that no matter how badly he thought he deserved it, he was not going to be allowed to headline over Run-DMC. "It wasn't possible," said Run. "You can't fly on the Wright Brothers forever. When the 747 came in, you had to ride right."

Adding insult to injury, Kurt was not only topped by his former student, he was replaced by his old partner—Grandmaster Flash. By this time, thanks to a whole ugly series of internal problems and management disputes, what had once been Grandmaster Flash & the Furious Five was now two different groups: Grandmaster Flash, and Grandmaster Melle Mel & the Furious Five.

And in a weird twist, one of the two original members of the Furious Five still remaining with Flash was Kid Creole, Mel's older brother. Mel was still recording for Sugarhill, but Flash had a contract with Elektra, one of the major labels. Thanks to the major's push and the built-in tastiness of the song itself, Flash had a hit that summer with a tune called "Larry's Dance." It was an instrumental (so much for Flash's new emcees) that used a machine called an emulator to stutter out "L-L-L-L-L-Larry"—precisely the kind of effect that flesh-and-blood hip-hop deejays, Flash certainly included, had pioneered years earlier.

Fresh Fest '85 was basically a bigger and better version of the first Fresh Fest, with the same mission—to make new fans for the artists involved. And, if Macon, Georgia is any indication, it succeeded. "Rap Music's Popularity Spreading to All Races, Ages," was the headline in the story in the *Macon Telegraph and News*. In an even more extravagant vein, Paul Peaghe, reviewing the show at New York's Nassau Coliseum, dubbed it, "the Woodstock of hip hop." It ran through

September 1, played arenas in 55 cities, and grossed more than $7 million.

But Run-D.M.C wasn't always reaching that MTV crowd, which is more suburban than city-based. So they stole a day from the Fresh Fest around June 12 and videotaped a concert especially for MTV at a rock club in New York called the Ritz. The show aired on the music channel on June 30 as a half-hour-long special entitled, appropriately enough, "Run-DMC Live At the Ritz." Critic Wayne Robins of *Newsday* wrote about what Run-DMC was achieving with such a show: "The crowd was the kind of cultural cross-section record companies dream about: everything from punks to preppies, lifeguards to b-boys, the ghetto kids by whom, for whom and about whom rap *was* initially."

The crew looked *ridiculously* All-American a few days later when the July issue of *Interview* magazine hit the streets. *Interview* was published by pop artist Andy Warhol in an oversized, 11-inch by 17-inch format, and mostly featured full-page black & white photos of the young and the beautiful or the rich and the famous, and of the blessed few who were young and beautiful *and* rich and famous. Although Run-DMC weren't yet rich and might never be beautiful, they were young and they were getting pretty famous, so there they were in *Interview*. They are posed as "The Spirit of '76," a reference to a very famous painting depicting battle-scarred American soldiers on the march during the Revolutionary War. There's D on the left in a tricorn hat and an old-fashioned vest, wearing his glasses as usual, with a snare drum slung around his neck and drumsticks in his hands. Jay's in the middle, propped up on a crutch, with a big white bandage tied around his forehead. And Run is on the right, dressed a lot like D and blowing into a fife. Behind them all is the American flag. Underneath, the caption reads: "Armed with fife, drum and flag, Yankee doodle rappers Run-DMC are seen here leaving the smoke of Yorktown behind, strains of 'It's Like That' in the air and revolution, the band's own credo, scratched into posterity." All right—it's hardly hiphop, but it is enthusiastic. And it did not hurt Run-DMC to be saluted by Andy Warhol.

❖ ❖ ❖

It all started with a Christmas record. Although he couldn't have known it at the time, Irish rocker Bob Geldof was kicking off a whole era of rock activism when he assembled a couple of dozen of the top English pop stars, dubbed them Band Aid, and cut a song called "Do They Know It's Christmas" in time for Christmas of 1984. The proceeds from the record were earmarked for African famine relief. "I thought the single would last two weeks, drop out of the charts, and I'd hand over the money to Save the Children," Geldof recalled in a recent interview. "But it didn't happen like that. Suddenly we had eight million pounds. Things went from there, and eventually there was Live Aid."

Specifically, "Do They Know It's Christmas" inspired a group of American superstar musicians led by Quincy Jones—including Michael Jackson, Bruce Springsteen, Stevie Wonder, Ray Charles, Diana Ross, Cyndi Lauper, and many others—to make a record called "We Are the World" under the name USA for Africa. And "We Are the World" led directly to the creation of Live Aid. Geldof announced the coming of Live Aid at a press conference held in Philadelphia on June 10, 1985. The event was set for July 13 and would consist of two concerts held simultaneously, one at Wembley Stadium in London, capacity 72,000, the other at JFK Stadium in Philadelphia, capacity 90,000—with both concerts beamed to a worldwide television audience of 1.5 *billion* people. Ninety percent of the countries in the world, including China and Russia, would receive it, 500 million of the 600 million homes with television, and millions more would receive the radio broadcast—and all of those people would be urged to pledge their money for the relief of the famine-stricken in Ethiopia. It was nothing short of colossal. It was, the press said, "the Woodstock of the Eighties."

One of the many remarkable things about Woodstock, however, was the racial diversity of the performers. If there is one image that has endured above all others since the hippies threw that psychedelic three-day bash for themselves in August of 1969, it is of Sly & the Family Stone thrilling half-a-million rockers of all colors with their rendition of "I Want to Take You Higher."

Now here was Bob Geldof announcing what stacked up to be a similarly influential event—and the press couldn't help but notice that only three of the 24 acts announced were black. Even weirder, it quickly turned out that Stevie Wonder, one of the three black acts announced as committed, had in fact declined to appear. Promoter Bill Graham, Geldof's partner in Live Aid, concocted a diplomatic dodge. "We all sometimes want things to work out so badly that there are no no's," he offered. "The worst that can be said is that honest mistakes were made."

Graham went on to say that "every major black artist on the *Billboard* Top 200 and black albums charts" had been approached, as had every black artist who had participated in the "We Are the World" recording session. "If they are not on the list of Live Aid performers," said Geldof, "you can draw your own conclusions." The implication was that Geldof had been in touch with dozens of black artists, and that only three of them had consented to be on the show. This story was ridiculous and the press immediately punched some holes in it. As just one example, Geldof had never asked Run-DMC to sign up, and the crew then had *two* albums in *Billboard*'s Top 200. In fact, Rush Productions had phoned Graham's office on Run-DMC's behalf as soon as Live Aid was announced, and were told, sorry, there is no more room on the bill.

Backpedaling now in the face of charges of racism, Geldof met the press again with a brand-new story. "My only criterion was whether the artist is currently popular and had the kind of recognition that would generate donations around the world," he said. "And this question about the black acts is preposterous. Would a racist go to all this trouble to keep these people alive? People who just happen to be black?" Pop music critic Ken Tucker of the *Philadelphia Inquirer* didn't buy any of it. "By any measure, Geldof's response . . . has been insensitive, if not downright stupid," he wrote. In addition, Tucker noted that on the basis of the great humanitarian's own standard, Geldof himself—whose most recent album had *not* cracked *Billboard*'s Top 200—should not have been on the bill.

Rolling Stone picked up picked up the story from there. "Thanks to his unique talent for saying the right thing in the wrong way at the most awkward time, Geldof managed to intensify the controversy. 'If you had a choice between seeing Chaka Khan and seeing the Who perform for one time only, who would *you* choose?' he asked a black reporter in Philadelphia."

Finally, however, Run-DMC were added to the bill. Having

learned that the Beach Boys, Madonna, and Tina Turner were added to the lineup *after* Run-DMC were told there was no more room, Rush Productions blew in another call to Bill Graham, who allowed that Run-DMC must have "somehow fallen between the cracks," and said, "We'll see you there!"

The final lineup consisted of 39 acts in Philly and 22 in London in a continuous event that went on for 16 hours. In addition to Run-DMC, such black acts as the Four Tops, Billy Ocean, Patti Labelle, Tina Turner (who performed with Mick Jagger), and David Ruffin and Eddie Kendricks (who performed with Hall & Oates) were there. And according to MTV newsman Tim Sommer, Mick Jagger had warmed up with Hall & Oates and their band on the evening before the show by running through . . . Run-DMC's "Rock Box."

Philadelphia was blazing hot on the day of the event itself, where the show was hosted by Jack Nicholson, Chevy Chase, and Joe Piscopo. Because of the number of acts on the bill, none was supposed to play more than two or three songs. There was a kind of giant turntable built right into the stage that could accommodate three acts at a time. While one act performed, two others were setting up out of sight of the audience. When the act performing was finished, the turntable was spun one-third of a turn so that the next act, all set up, suddenly faced the audience, ready to roll. This one innovation really kept things moving.

Run-DMC, then on tour with the Fresh Fest, had played the night before Live Aid in Savannah, Georgia. On Saturday morning, the day of the show, they took a chartered plane to Atlanta and then flew to Philadelphia, where Live Aid traffic had made the streets virtually impassable. The crew was whisked straight from the airport to the stadium by a police escort with sirens blaring, and even then they made it to the stage with only a few minutes to spare.

They ended up nestled snugly between a reunion performance by heavy metalists Ozzy Osbourne and Black Sabbath and a set by Rick Springfield, who had leapt to pop stardom from his perch as a regular on a daytime television soap opera. The world's premier rap trio turned in the most ferocious six-minute show of their career between 10:18 and 10:24a.m. The reaction from the nearly all-white crowd, wrote *Billboard* columnist Brian Chin, was "polite." He added that the crowd was "mellow enough until mid-afternoon, after which time they demanded the goods pretty persistently. ('Where's the Boss?' questioned one banner.)" The crew then met the press and jumped back on a plane to Macon, Georgia, where they rejoined the Fresh Fest.

Unfortunately, the folks watching the action at home weren't given much of a chance to see Run-DMC. As critic Robert Palmer put it in the *New York Times*, "MTV gave critics who accuse it of racism another round of ammunition when it cut off the black rap group Run-DMC after a snippet of a single song in order not to miss a verbose introduction for Sting's performance at Wembley."

MTV's John Sykes, a white man, shrugged it off. "We missed white acts, we missed black acts," he ho-hummed. "We weren't swayed either way." Bob Pittman, the head of programming for MTV—and Sykes' boss—claimed that there had been no oversight, and that Run's brief set hadn't been aired because of a technical screw-up. "Although we had planned on airing Run-DMC after 11pm, at the last minute we discovered the tape provided by [the producers] earlier in the day had no audio," he wrote in a gracious letter to Russell.

"If you have a tape of the performance, we would like to include it in an upcoming recap of the event. We are excited about Run-DMC. Let's keep the momentum rolling."

But the momentum, at least concerning the actual Live Aid telecast, had been lost. Whether it was because of racism, color-blind bad taste or technical error, Run-DMC had been denied exposure on the single biggest television broadcast in history. And truthfully, for all their concern about the cause behind Live Aid, Run-DMC was also interested in that unprecedented exposure—just as were all the other acts on the bill.

But there's no question that the event was a fund-raising success—$120 million was the figure by the end of 1986. Likewise, there's no question but that Run-DMC was right to fight to get on the bill, nor any doubt that the event benefitted by their presence. They were the *only* act at Live Aid that appealed to black teens—and to the extent that the event was dedicated to *educating* people about this terrible problem as well as about raising money, Run-DMC was essential. Or as Jam Master Jay pointed out, "It was an important cause, but without us involved, a whole lot of kids wouldn't have known or cared about it at all."

❖ ❖ ❖

Early on the morning of August 3, 1985, Run-DMC taped a performance on Dick Clark's "American Bandstand" for broadcast on August 24. They were the first rap group ever to appear on the pioneering rock music television show—and it was about time. Run-DMC now had two gold albums to their credit. They'd put five singles into the Black Top 20. They'd played at Live Aid. Their videos were on MTV. They were selling out arenas across the country. And they were about to debut in their first movie. In fact, there may have been no better indication that "Bandstand" was ready for Run-DMC than the wild cheering of the fresh-faced, blond-haired southern Californians in the studio audience when the crew walked onstage. The group busted out "King of Rock" and then "Jam Master Jammin'"—and not the one on the *King of Rock* album, but a new version featuring the rip-roaring guitar of Rick Rubin.

Afterward, they walked around behind the set for a picture or two with Dick Clark, the man they call the world's oldest teenager. Dick was friendly, but at first he posed with Run-DMC in the same way he poses with everybody: he smiled, but he was a little distant. Run-DMC convinced him instead to "chill" in a b-boy stance, arms folded across his chess, his head pulled back, looking mean. Or at least "mean." It was a great shot, and magazines all across the country printed it.

Not long after Live Aid, Run-DMC were approached by a rock musician named Little Steven Van Zandt to contribute to an anti-apartheid record he was producing. Steven had first come to international attention as the lead guitarist with Bruce Springsteen's E Street Band, and Springsteen still referred to Steven as "my best friend." The soft-spoken but intensely political rocker went out on his own in 1983 as the leader of a band called the Disciples of Soul. Steven's political interests eventually led him to visit South Africa, to investigate first-hand the system of apartheid, or state-sponsored racism, that had long before inspired the United Nations to call for a world-wide cultural and sports boycott of that country.

South Africa is a country of 23 million people where the black population outnumbers the white by a margin of five to one. Apartheid is the system that keeps the white minority in power. Under its laws South Africa's black citizens are forbidden to vote, to buy or sell land in most parts of the country, to choose where to live or work, or to travel freely. It is, in sum, a system of modern slavery under which a black citizen has no freedom or civil rights.

As an artist of conscience, Steven was naturally revolted by what he saw of apartheid, and when he asked the South Africans he met what he, as an American musician, could do to help them to overthrow the system, they told him to tell his friends and colleagues in the music industry not to play Sun City.

Sun City is a perfect symbol of apartheid, a $90 million pleasure resort for the rich and privileged in the middle of the vast rural slum of surrounding Bophuthatswana, which is one of the so-called "independent homelands" of South Africa. According to "Sun City: The Making of the Record" by Dave Marsh, Sun City features "a casino, an artificial lake, softporn movies, discotheques, and scantily clad chorus girls" as part of an enormous complex that also boasts a superbowl—which is "a large auditorium that regularly attracts big-name international entertainers and athletes, lured there by exorbitant fees and South Africa's assurances that the audience is not part of the apartheid system.

"In reality, living conditions are harsh for the blacks who have been forcibly relocated to Bophuthatswana, and independence from apartheid and South Africa is merely an illusion." Tickets to events at Sun City are usually far too expensive for the black citizens of Bophuthatswana to afford, so a few token tickets are often given away so that the entertainers can perform before a "mixed" audience.

Despite offers of millions of dollars to play Sun City, such artists and athletes as Stevie Wonder, Gladys Knight & the Pips, Billy Ocean, the Harlem Globetrotters, and John McEnroe have refused. Others, such as Frank Sinatra, Tina Turner, the O'Jays, Queen, Linda Ronstadt, Rod Stewart, and Elton John have defied the boycott, taken the money, and played Sun City.

Steven and his partner on the project, producer Arthur Baker (who'd made records with Afrika Bambaataa, Bruce Springsteen, and Cyndi Lauper) simply hoped that their record—which was entitled "Sun City"—would "hurt Sun City's ability to lure entertainers." They also hoped that "by focusing on South Africa and its exaggerated racism, we can realize that racism is very much alive in our country and other countries of the world. It is very important that we take responsibility and action to dismantle our own apartheid right here at home." The song's punchline was, "I ain't gonna play Sun City."

As to what, in the words of *Jet* magazine, "a nice New Jersey white boy" like Steven was doing orchestrating an anti-apartheid anthem, Steven replied, "My mama taught me a lot of things when I was growing up, but she forgot to teach me that I was white. Life for me," he added, "is divided into people who have freedom and people who don't—regardless of color."

The all-star lineup for "Sun City" was racially and musically diverse by design. The song itself featured rap verses and a sung chorus. Although the final lineup of the group that came to be called the Artists United Against Apartheid included such superstars and legends as Bruce Springsteen, Miles Davis, Ruben Blades, Jimmy Cliff, George Clinton, Bob Dylan, Peter Gabriel, Hall & Oates, Herbie Hancock, Bonnie Raitt, Joey Ramone, Keith Richards and Ron Wood of the Rolling Stones, Lou Reed, and Gil Scott-Heron, "the first people we contacted who were very supportive," noted Steven, "were the New York rappers." And the first of those to jump in were Run-DMC.

"We gave no consideration whatsoever as to how successful somebody was, just how soulful," Steve said. "Every artist was equally important to us—it's just that some of them sell lots of records and some of them don't."

It was, by the way, much riskier commercially for an artist to get involved with a record like "Sun City," which directly criticized President Ronald Reagan's support of the South African government, than it was to get involved with a good cause like "We Are the World," which aimed to fight hunger, but which didn't step on any powerful toes. And it was riskier still to get involved at the very beginning of such a project, well before superstars like Springsteen took the plunge. But, as Steven put it, "We as an industry have spoken out on starvation. It is time to speak out on the hunger for freedom."

Run agreed. "It's important that young people know about the situation in South Africa, and we figured we can use our voices to make sure apartheid won't go on forever. We wouldn't go and play there no matter what they paid." Steven and Run-DMC were introduced to each other by television news producer Danny Schechter, who'd met Russell in the summer of 1981 while preparing a story on rap—featuring Kurtis Blow—for ABC-TV's "20/20." Shortly thereafter, Rush artists Kurtis Blow and Scorpio (formerly of the Furious Five) joined the project, as did rappers Melle Mel, Afrika Bambaataa, Duke Bootee, the Fat Boys, and Jamaica's Big Youth. It's no accident that the very first line of "Sun City" reads: "We're rockers and rappers united and strong"—nor that Run-DMC are the rockers who rap it.

The crew cut their part at Arthur Baker's Shakedown Studios in Manhattan on a hot day in August. Early in October they joined Kurtis and Scorpio and the rest of the rappers uptown in Harlem to shoot part of the video that was made for "Sun City," and on October 10 they joined up with the whole huge "Sun City" crew—50-odd artists, including Springsteen—for a video shoot in Washington Square Park in Greenwich Village. A team effort featuring such important film and video directors as Jonathan Demme, Godley & Creme, and Hart Perry, the video was superb.

But even given the high quality of the "Sun City" record and video, Steven had a very rough time finding a label for the project. "The record labels told me that rock and politics don't mix," he recalled. After finally placing "Sun City" with Manhattan Records, Steven was able to prove that those other companies had been wrong. Although Steven's purpose had indeed been political, "Sun City" did well in the marketplace. Released on October 30, the record eventually broke into the Top 40 on *Billboard*'s Hot 100 singles chart, and climbed to number 21 on the Black Singles chart. (All proceeds went to the Africa Fund, a charitable trust that aids political prisoners and their families in South Africa.) More impressively, it was chosen the number one single of the year by the *New York Times*. Most impressively, it was honored in a ceremony at the United Nations, attended by Run-DMC, at which UN Secretary General Javier Perez de Cuellar said, "'Sun City' is an affirmation of the resolve of artists to awaken the public to the true nature of apartheid and to put an end to this inhuman and totally unacceptable policy."

All in all, and especially with regard to the howl that came from the South African government—which effectively, if not officially, banned the record—it was clear that "Sun City" was a job well done.

It wasn't long after Run-DMC finished with "Sun City" that they signed on to help make another all-star benefit record, this one honoring the memory of Dr. Martin Luther King. This benefit was the brainchild of Dexter King, at 24 the youngest son of Dr. King and Coretta Scott King. The first national observance of the King holiday was set for January 15, 1986—just a couple of months down the road—and Dexter was worried that "the post-civil rights generation doesn't really understand what my father's teachings meant, and how they changed the whole tone of this nation."

Dexter—who looks a *lot* like his father—was still a student at Morehouse College in Atlanta, where he did a little deejaying on the side. And if there was one thing Dexter understood about today's teens, it is that rap music is the way to reach them. "Rap music," he believed, "just clicks."

Dexter's first thought was to reach out to "the King of Rap" himself—Mr. Kurtis Blow, who ended up co-producing the song that would be entitled "King Holiday."

Kurt brought Run-DMC aboard, and Whodini too. Once word of the project got around, however, a whole raft of significant artists signed up, all of them under 30 years of age. They included New Edition, Whitney Houston, Stacy Lattisaw, James "JT" Taylor of Kool & the Gang, El Debarge, Lisa Lisa and Full Force, Menudo, Stephanie Mills, and Teena Marie (who collectively comprised "the King Dream Chorus,")—as well as Melle Mel and the Fat Boys, who, along with Kurt, Run, and Whodini comprised the Holiday Crew.

Built of both rapped and sung parts, the song began with the following rap:

> Once a year we celebrate/Washington and Lincoln on their birthdates
> And now a third name is added to this list/A man of peace, "the Drum Major for Justice"
> Now every January on the third Monday/We pay homage to the man who paved the way
> For freedom, justice and equality/To make the world a better place for you and me
> It's a holiday! It's a gathering! For the Reverend Dr. Martin Luther King!

The sung part of the song drives home one of its most important messages: "He had a dream, now it's up to you/To see it through, to make it come true."

Kurt, naturally enough, was thrilled when it was finished. "I think it's the most important project of our time, even more important than 'We Are the World' or 'Sun City,'" he said. "It's about something happening right here in America and about one of the biggest heroes of American history." Unfortunately, Polygram Records, the firm that was distributing the record, didn't agree that the project was quite as momentous as all that, and refused to cough up the money to make a music video. To the rescue came Prince, who hadn't been able to get involved with the project earlier because he'd been in France filming "Under the Cherry Moon." The freaky young funkster, still at the height of his popularity in the aftermath of the multiplatinum success of the "Purple Rain" album and film, donated $85,000 for that very purpose, and the video was duly produced.

Between November 27 and December 8, 1985 Run-DMC

headlined another little foray into the precincts of pure pop, this one called the Rock and Rule Tour. Unlike the Fresh Fest, which played ten thousand-seat arenas, this tour was routed through rock clubs, places like the Front Row Theater in Highland Heights, Ohio, the Inferno in Buffalo, New York, and the Channel in Boston. And, indeed, it was a "rock" tour, with Fishbone and the Red Hot Chili Peppers filling out the bill. The tests for this lineup were shows the previous September at the Warfield Theater in San Francisco and the Hollywood Palladium in Los Angeles. Don Waller of the *Los Angeles Times* reviewed the show at the four thousand-seat Palladium: "The pair threw down 45 minutes of their finest rhymes with the white-hot intensity of down-home gospel preachers. Backed solely by turntable wizard Jam Master Jay, this ultra-*moderne* version of '60s soul men Sam & Dave gave the mostly teen-age, multiracial crowd a lean, mean stream of couplets that stretched from state-of-the-ghetto message tunes to ground-breaking metal-funk fusion."

Waller also applauded "equally imaginative, manic sets from the two opening acts: young white metalfunkheads the Red Hot Chili Peppers and young black ska-punk-funkateers Fishbone. So who won this battle of the bands? The audience."

Just before Christmas of 1985 Run-DMC rejoined most of the King Dream Chorus and Holiday Crew at the Martin Luther King Jr. Center for Non-Violent Social Change in Atlanta (the beneficiary of the proceeds of the "King Holiday" project) to film the video of the record. Mrs. King was in the house, as was Andrew Young, the mayor of Atlanta, and both of them expressed their thanks to the artists at length—and "King Holiday" was released a few weeks later, just in time for the first King Holiday.

The following year Run-DMC would pay personal tribute to Dr. King in their record "Proud to Be Black"—"What's wrong with you, man? How could you be so dumb? Like Dr. King said, 'We shall overcome!'"—but just now the crew felt honored to be part of this praiseworthy group effort. Certainly as far as Dexter King was concerned, "King Holiday" had accomplished its mission. "The lyrics tell you to put your hate away, in an official living memorial to my father's ideals," he said. "Those who don't know the impact of the civil rights movement will be educated, while those of us who do know will be reminded."

Amen.

EIGHT

Raising Hell

Run-DMC spent the first several months of 1986 working on the album that would be called *Raising Hell*. It is by far the best album of their career, very possibly because for the first time they largely produced it themselves. That is, not only did they write and rap all the rhymes, they composed virtually all of the music and recorded it (with the expert help of engineer Steve Ett) as well. With the notable exception of "Walk This Way," the crew did their work in the studio and took the results to Russell and Rick, the nominal co-producers, who'd sit there and listen to the playback, look at each other and shrug, and agree that the jam was finished, just as it was.

A lot of pressure comes with that much responsibility, but the crew felt there was no other way to get the job done. "*King of Rock* wasn't as good as we wanted. It wasn't the best Run-DMC could do," said Jay. "So we produced this one ourselves. We wanted it to be def, and it is."

Super-competitive Run saw the challenge in his own terms. He said that during the winter prior to the release of *Raising Hell*, he'd "turn off the tv because all I saw was LL Cool J. All I heard on the radio was LL Cool J. Oh, my god! It was like I was Richard Pryor and he was Eddie Murphy!" Likewise, after the album was finished but before it was released, Run said: "Everybody is looking for us to go downhill now. If we come with another weak album, we could be over with. So we went to work."

Jay had a good fix on the way the group worked together. "Run comes up with the initial idea, D writes most of the rest of the record, then I'll come up with the music and arrange it," he said. "Then we put it all together. No one of us has the formula. We all have it." Run thinks of the method as each of the guys contributing thirty-three-and-a-third percent to the unity that is Run-DMC.

The recording was done at Chung King, "the House of Metal," a funky little studio on the sixth floor of a building on Centre Street in that part of lower Manhattan where Little Italy, Chinatown, and Soho all come together. It is owned by partners John "Chung" King and Steve Ett, who opened the studio in 1983 more as a hobby than a business. Accordingly, they called it Secret Society then, and concentrated on making their own records. However, they'd bought state-of-the-art equipment, and pretty soon found themselves renting out studio time for productions by new wave rockers like Soviet Sex, Certain Generals, and the Rattlers—all of whom appreciated the high sound quality and the low cost, and who didn't mind that the place had none of the creature comforts of the more luxurious midtown studios.

It was Rick Rubin who discovered Chung King for hiphop

purposes and, beginning in 1984, with the Beastie Boys' "Rock Hard," nearly all of the singles released by Def Jam when it was still an independent label were cut there—as have been subsequent albums by LL Cool J, the Beastie Boys, and Oran "Juice" Jones.

The first side of *Raising Hell* kicks off with Run-DMC writing themselves into the Mother Goose nursery rhymes book:

> Now Peter Piper picked peppers, but Run rocks rhymes
> Humpty Dumpty fell down, that's his hard times
> Jack B. Nimble was nimble and he was quick
> But Jam Master is faster. Jack's on Jay's dick

The music makes use of the carnival-style break from pop jazz pianist Bob James's recording of "Mardi Gras," which had long since established itself as a break-beat classic.

"It's Tricky" is a rocker that combines the guitar from the Knack's "My Sharona" with the rhythms of Toni Basil's "Mickey." Run conceived of the track as a way to muse on rap's outlaw status. "I was telling people who think that rapping is something that anyone can do that they're wrong," he said. "We don't get Grammies, but we sell millions of records, more than a lot of singers, and we don't get the respect we deserve. I came up with a lyric: 'They say I'm overrated, musicians really hate it/My name is Run, I'm number one, it's very complicated.'"

"It's Tricky" also contains an anti-drug message which, Run wrote "*consciously,* because I know kids are listening, and they have to know about that." The rhyme runs as follows: "We are not thugs, we don't use drugs, but you assume on your own/They offer dope and lots of coke, but we just leave it alone." It's a verse that came in handy during that summer's tour, when conservative critics, focusing on the group's tough image but neglecting to listen to music's lyrics, insisted that Run-DMC's music incited kids to violence.

"My Adidas" is a pure love song to the crew's favorite footwear. Run-DMC had no endorsement deal with the manufacturer at the time—although the song did lead to a deal. "We started wearing them back in 1978 when they first brought out the shell-toe style—where the toe looks like a sea shell," D recalls. "As it says in the song, 'I like to sport them, that's why I bought them.'" Jam Master Jay claims that the crew wrote the song because younger kids were asking Run-DMC why they still wore Adidas when everybody else had moved on to Reeboks, Fila and Troops. But a close look at the lyrics reveals that the song isn't about Run-DMC's footwear exactly, but what they've accomplished while wearing them:

> My Adidas!
> Walked through concert doors, and roamed all over coliseum floors
> I stepped onstage at Live Aid. All the people gave and the poor got paid
> And out of speakers I did speak. I wore my sneakers, but I'm not a sneak
> My Adidas touched the sands of foreign lands, with mike in hand I cold took command
> My Adidas and me, close as can be, we make a mean team, my Adidas and me.

One of the album's great standouts is "Perfection," a real relaxed and funny rhyme driven hard by live drums, which feels as if it had been recorded back in Run's attic at the end of a long night. In fact, it was recorded live in one take at

Chung King with a 16-year-old drummer from Hollis named Sticks. Run in particular is in a playful mood—he raps his part in a cartoonish falsetto—as he and D take their patented teamwork to new heights:

D: I got bass
Run: Tone!
D: I use
Run: Cologne!
D: And then I rock a funky rhyme on the micro-
Run: phone!
D: I got a funky fresh
Run: car!
D: With a funky fresh
Run: bar!
D: I'm a funky fresh
Run: star!
D: And I'm up to
Run: par!
D: My name is DM
Run: C!
D: Down the Run and
Run: Jay!
D: Is everything copasetic, y'all?
Run: A-Okay!
Both: Perfection!

Side two begins with "Hit It Run," which may be the album's wildest and most energetic song. In it Run debuts his "human beat box" arsenal of mouth rhythms, featuring techniques pioneered by Doug E. Fresh and the Fat Boys' Darren "Buffy" Robinson. D begins the song without any musical accompaniment, in a deliberate echo of "King of Rock," and then has all the rhymes to himself:

Do you really believe what's going on?
I was conceived and I was born
I once was lost, but now I'm found
Tell your bunch I'm boss. I run this town
I leave all suckers in the dust
Those dumb motherfuckers can't mess with us
Beats flow from Joe and never stop
You'd better get yourself together
Let's rock!

And rock Run does, transforming himself into a self-described "human breath box," whose funky splutterings and gaspings add up to a whole new bag of tricks.

Next comes the title track, "Raising Hell," five-and-a-half minutes of heavy-metal mashing. As with "It's Tricky," hysterical adults pointed to the title of this tune during the summer of '86 as "evidence" that Run-DMC were not simply evil, they were Satanists—as if "raising hell" hadn't always meant having plain old harmless fun. Indeed, the crew's critics had it completely backward: This is a song that finds Run-DMC "*dissing* all devils" and "causing havoc in hell." In sum, it's the closest the crew has ever come to writing a gospel song.

"You Be Illin'" might be the funniest song on a very funny album. With its vignettes of weird characters ordering hamburgers at a chicken restaurant and shouting "Touchdown!" at basketball games, and its one-fingered piano part and chuckling sax, it is reminiscent of nothing so much as great novelty records from the Fifties like The Coasters's "Charlie Brown."

"Dumb Girl" is about one girl, not all girls, a girl who lies and gets high and who gives "every guy a try at the wink of an eye." It is an attempt to knock some sense into this person's head before it's too late.

"Son of Byford" is twenty-seven seconds' worth of studio silliness—the great last verse of "Hit it Run" busted out grandly by D, accompanied by Run's blustery beat box, for the amusement of Jay.

The most serious song on the album is "Proud to Be Black," *Raising Hell*'s "It's Like That." Written by DMC, Run's father Daniel, and Andre "Dr. Dre" Brown of Original Concept, it makes a whirlwind tour of the great achievers in African-American history—Harriet Tubman, Martin Luther King, Malcolm X, George Washington Carver, Jesse Owens—and ends up talking about . . . Run-DMC:

> I want to tell you something put your mind in a swirl
> God bless the next baby that comes in this world
> A world full of hate, discrimination and sin
> People judging other people by the color of skin
> I'll take this matter in my own way
> Man, I ain't no slave. I ain't baling no hay
> We're in a tight position in any condition
> Don't get in my way 'cause I'm full of ambition
> I'm proud to be black and I ain't taking no crap
> I'm fresh out the pack, and I'm proud to be black
> So take that!

The remaining track is another of *Raising Hell*'s standouts. The album was nearly finished when Rick suggested that the crew record their own version of "Walk This Way," a song originally cut by the Boston-based rock band Aerosmith for a 1976 album entitled *Toys in the Attic*.

It was an inspired idea. Run-DMC's affection for that particular recording went back to the time of its initial release, when Jay and Run and dozens of other hiphop deejays used to cut the tune's hard and funky drum pattern —boom *bash*, b-b-boom *bash*—back and forth from one turntable to the next, as hopeful young emcees-in-training worked out the kinks in their new rhymes undistracted by anything but that beat. In a word, it had been an absolute b-boy classic for ten years. Likewise, it was certainly a natural choice for someone with Rick's background. Aerosmith was his favorite band as a teenager. It was also Rick's idea to ask Steven Tyler and Joe Perry, the band's lead singer and lead guitarist, respectively, to join Run-DMC on the new recording.

Joe Perry later confessed that he was "a little surprised" when he got the call asking him to record with Run, although he further confessed that he'd already been inadvertently exposed to rap when he heard it come "blaring out" of the bedroom of his 13-year-old stepson. "It was new. It was *fresh*, in the rap sense of the term," he said. "I didn't go out and buy a bunch of rap records, but I did get a sense of what was going on there."

Given their radical hiphop editing of the record "back in the days," Run-DMC had to confess some ignorance of their own. "We didn't know about 'back seat lover who's always undercover,' but when we started listening to the record, we started liking it," said Run. This is his way of saying that, prior to recording, he didn't know any of the tune's lyrics. For that matter, up until they met for the first time, Run-DMC didn't even really know the correct name of the Boston band. "It was the funniest thing in the world," recalled Russell. "They kept talking about 'my homeboy Steve from Toys in the Attic!'"

The session was held in New York at the Magic Venture

Studios on March 9, 1986. Tyler and Perry flew up for it from Philadelphia. Aerosmith had played the night before to a sold-out crowd at Philadelphia's Spectrum, which just happens to be where Run plays when *they're* in the City of Brotherly Love. "I didn't know Run from DMC and they didn't know Steven from me at the beginning of the session," Perry said. "But we cracked a lot of beers and had a lot of fun that day." The feeling was mutual. "Joe and Steve's my best friends," Jay said later. "They're like old homeboys."

The recording itself proceeded pretty casually. "When I first walked into the studio I didn't know what was gonna happen," Perry said. "I thought they would have had some definite ideas on how they were going to rearrange the song, but all they had was a drum track. Then Rick Rubin came up to me and said, 'Just play the song the way you play it.' So I put down a guitar track, and then Steven went into the vocal booth with Run and DMC, and they just rapped their way through the song. It was done in five hours and we all enjoyed the end result."

What's not to enjoy? Run-DMC's version of "Walk This Way" is a virtual duplicate of the original, with the addition of Run and DMC's vocals. The obvious comfort that both groups feel for the material supports Rick's contention that "the only wall between rock and rap is racism"—a point underscored by the great video made of the song by director Jon Small.

The video starts out with Aerosmith and Run-DMC in adjoining rehearsal studios. Aerosmith is playing "Walk This Way" so loudly that it disturbs Run-DMC in the next room. Run-DMC decides to fight fire with fire and play their own loud version of "Walk This Way," with Jay mischievously scratching away. Now Aerosmith is pissed off. The two groups hammer away at the wall separating them, trying to get the other posse to shut up, when suddenly that wall comes tumbling down. Next thing you know Run and D and Steven are onstage performing the song *together* (in a scene shot at the Park Theater in Union City, New Jersey) to the obvious delight of a houseful of heaving rock fans.

All in all, Run-DMC ended up making both MTV and rock radio an offer they couldn't refuse. Along with Led Zeppelin's "Stairway to Heaven" and very few others, "Walk This Way" was one of the songs that *defined* FM rock radio. It had been played constantly on the format for ten straight years—and now here were the guys who cut the original performing on a sizzling new version, thus putting their stamp of approval on it. In fact, the song became an across-the-board smash. It not only went to number eight on the Black Singles chart, it went to number *four* on the Hot 100, which was the first time Run-DMC had ever appeared on that chart.

There was, predictably, some backlash. "I've had a couple people come up to me and say, 'Don't you think this is gonna do something to your heavy-metal image?' Perry recalled. "I had to say, '*What* heavy-metal image? We're an r&b band. This is just a little side thing that Steven and I, having written the song, decided to do for some fun. If that bothers you, then you've got a bigger problem than us by far.'"

In fact, *Kerrang!*, England's monthly bible of heavy-metal, went so far as to put Aerosmith and Run-DMC on their cover—even as their reviewer was expressing his amazement at just how much he and his colleagues dug the collaboration: "God knows how the thing got past our security guards and into the office, but the fact is that it did, and within minutes it had transformed some of the toughest Metal men in all of

Camden into Hip Hop hotheads." Apparently the gospel according to Run-DMC is tougher than *metal*, too. "Music is music, good's good," decreed the Reverend Run. "You laugh at Rodney Dangerfield. You laugh at Eddie Murphy. Let's not call it black or white."

All of a sudden it looked like lots of people were coming around to that open-minded point of view—and if the walls weren't actually tumbling down, they were definitely crumbling at the corners. Consider the New York Music Awards. Organized by New Yorkers who believe that the Grammys, which are held every year in Los Angeles, reflect a West Coast bias, the first annual New York Music Awards show was held on March 29, 1986 at the four thousand-seat Felt Forum. According to the votes cast for this show, Run-DMC wasn't just a great *rap* act, they were among the best acts of any category in the music business, and certainly among the very best from New York. The crew was nominated in five categories and won in four—Best Single ("King of Rock"), Best Song ("King of Rock"—a songwriter's award), Best R&B Act, and Best Rap Act. This was as many awards as were won by Whitney Houston (a much more conventional act), and more than almost every other act nominated—including the Talking Heads. In the 1986 awards, held on April 4, 1987, Run-DMC walked away with the top award—Outstanding Group of the Year—winning over the Talking Heads, the Ramones, and Cameo.

With the summer of 1986 looming, it was time to start planning the third annual Fresh Fest. This time, however, Rush Productions and Ricky Walker weren't able to reach an agreement about the money. Negotiating for Rush was Lyor Cohen, who'd joined Rush in February 1985 and has been a kind of acting vice-president of operations ever since.

Lyor was and is a remarkable character. A brief first meeting with him might leave you wondering if he's retarded. He's very tall, about six-foot-five, with a big square head and a manner of speech that combines a hard-to-place dialect with the tendency to mangle most metaphors. In the beginning Run-DMC found Lyor's basic style so goofy that they bestowed two equally ridiculous nicknames on him. They called him Herman, after tv's Frankensteinian head Munster, and "Girallama," a Dr. Seuss-like neologism which amalgamated Lyor's giraffe-like height and his llama-like awkwardness.

Physical quirks aside, Lyor is both smart and very tough. The child of Israelis, he grew up in Los Angeles and earned a degree in international finance and marketing from the University of Miami. His first job out of school was as a shrimp farmer in Ecuador. Then he worked as a financial analyst at the National Bank of Israel in Beverly Hills, a job he hated and quit.

At the age of 23 Lyor decided to go into show business. He borrowed a thousand dollars from his mother, partnered up with some Koreans, and opened a nightclub called the Mix Club. The building had been known for years and years as the Stardust Ballroom, having opened in the Thirties to accomodate the craze for the fox trot. During the Seventies it was reborn as a punk palace that didn't last. When Lyor got his hands on it in 1983, his booking policy was "all the music that other promoters wouldn't touch"—rap, punk, and reggae. He ran the club for two years and, with the self-effacing modesty for which he is widely admired, he says, "I made a fortune."

His very first show featured Run-DMC at the top of a bill that also included the Circle Jerks, Fear, Social Distortion,

Fishbone, and the Red Hot Chili Peppers. Tickets were $10 each, and Lyor packed 3500 people into a club that held 3000—which means that he ended up grossing $35,000 on a show that cost him maybe $10,000.

The only trouble was that the headliners never appeared. Or rather, that they showed up way too late. Run-DMC, then traveling for some reason with no road manager, had played three other gigs in Los Angeles that night. When they finally rolled into the Mix Club at six a.m., Jay told Lyor, "If you got the cash, we'll go on." Lyor waved his hand in the direction of the empty club, and said, "This is Los Angeles. We've been closed for two hours."

To apologize for their botched first gig, the crew returned to the Mix Club several times, making a lot of friends in the process. By June 16, 1984—when Run-DMC headlined over the Dickies, the Red Hot Chili Peppers, Fishbone, Cathedral of Tears, and the Cambridge Apostles—Lyor had succeeded in making the Mix Club a definite Hollywood hotspot. As the *L.A. Weekly* put it in its preview of that show, "Never before has such a churning Hollywood funhouse of fashionable faces and hard-edged rhymes been accumulated in one ballroom. If the groove bone in your body needs oiling, this is the place for the rhythm and lube job."

Six months later, however, Lyor decided that New York City, the home of Rush Productions, was the place to be. Accordingly, he packed his bags and simply showed up at 1133 Broadway, insisting that the flabbergasted Russell put him to work. In fact, Russell wasn't really paying anything in the way of salaries at the time, which meant that his small staff was forced to operate as a kind of loose confederacy of hustlers: When and if you generated business for any of the Rush artists, you were awarded a percentage of that business.

This arrangement suited Lyor to the bone. "I'm gonna make you more money in merchandising and tours and everything else than you ever make on your records," he promised Run.

By the spring of 1986, Lyor was handling most of the financial affairs for Rush. It was no problem not coming to an agreement with Ricky Walker. Jeff Sharp's Stageright Productions, out of Lutherville, Maryland, and Darryll Brooks and Carol Kirkendall's G Street Express, out of Washington, D.C., would be the new tour's national co-promoters. G Street had promoted George Clinton's Parliament/Funkadelic mob for five years, Stageright had handled Prince and Luther Vandross nationally, and the two companies had worked together before on individual dates.

The idea this time was no Fat Boys and no breakdancers. It would be just Rush, ruling—Run-DMC, Whodini, LL Cool J, and the Beastie Boys—Ladies and Gentlemen, the Raising Hell Tour. It was, no question, a powerhouse line-up. Run-DMC's *Raising Hell,* sitting on advance orders for six hundred thousand copies, would be released one week before the start of the tour, and go on to sell over a million copies in its first five weeks, quickly making it the first album by rappers ever to achieve platinum status. Whodini had sold damn near a million copies of their previous album, and released their new one, *Back in Black* (another Larry Smith production), just a few weeks prior to the start of the tour. Immediately, "Funky Beat," the first single, began to rocket up the Black Singles chart. LL Cool J's first album, *Radio,* had been released in time for "Krush Groove" the previous fall. Seven months later the eighteen-year-old had a gold record and several hit singles to his credit, including "I Can't

Live Without My Radio," "Rock the Bells," and "You'll Rock."

The Beastie Boys, meanwhile, had opened for Madonna on her summer of 1985 Virgin Tour, perhaps the most spectacular tour mismatch since the aborted Monkees/Jimi Hendrix Experience team-up in 1967. She'd asked her old pal Russell for Run-DMC, but Russ told her Run was already too big to open for anyone else—and suggested the Beasties instead. It defied belief that this trio of unknown, pimply, rap-spouting punks could occupy the same planet with the goddess Madonna, let alone the same bill—but Madonna went for it.

The Beasties immediately grasped the comic possibilities in this opportunity, and made sure that they lived up to their name. Every night for three months they stood in front of ten thousand 12-year-old Madonna-wanna-be's and cursed, drank beer, grabbed their crotches, and pushed each other around—and then, as the confusion and the revulsion rose and the boos thundered down, they'd stalk the stage with their fists held over their heads, bathing in it all like 98-pound bad-guy wrestlers.

On the last date of the tour, at Madison Square Garden in New York, the Beasties and Madonna's band cooked up a little surprise for the star of the show. When she came running back onto the stage for her encore wearing nothing on top but a see-through bra, as she did every night, all the guys in her band dropped their pants to reveal ridiculous red-and-white polka-dot boxer shorts. While Madonna stood there gaping in disbelief, the Beasties charged onto the stage wearing the same kind of shorts—and firing water pistols at the Queen. She ran off in mock terror.

Now it was a year later and time for Russell to put into

action his original plan for the Beasties, which was to "break them" to a black audience first, and then to cross them over to a white audience. "Otherwise," he reasoned, "they'll just be these fake white rappers." Russ had tested this tactic a few times before with the Beasties, having them open for Kurtis Blow in front of an all-black audience at a club in Queens called the Encore, for example. That night, early in 1985, it didn't work, and they were booed offstage.

By the summer of 1986 and the commencement of the Raising Hell Tour, however, the Beastie Boys were much better performers. They'd prance onto the stage doing an idiot dance called the Jerry Lewis, run through records like "Slow and Low" (co-written with Run) and "Hold It Now, Hit It" (which was a hit on the Black Singles chart that summer, but which did not cross over) and run off 15 minutes later. If the largely black crowds were momentarily put off by the sight of these three skinny white guys taking the stage, they were also quickly won over by the def jams and deffer rapping. Every night, just as Russell intended, the Beastie Boys proved that they were no joke.

The Raising Hell Tour kicked off in Columbus, Georgia on May 21, and roared along for over a month with no problems. By June 21, with "My Adidas" well on its way into the Black Singles Top 5, Run could ask the sell-out crowd of 20,000 hiphop heads at Philadelphia's Spectrum to show him their Adidas and get five thousand pairs immediately thrust up into the air.

Now actively in pursuit of an endorsement deal for Run-DMC from the manufacturers of these shoes, Lyor filmed this passionate little display of brand loyalty and sent it to his contacts at Adidas, along with reports of what had happened at Run-DMC's in-store appearance at an Adidas outlet in Baltimore on June 27—when 13,000 kids showed up and the entire mall had to be shut down.

The next night, in Pittsburgh, after 24 trouble-free shows in six weeks, the tour finally hit a snag. Or rather, there was trouble *after* the show, which was held at the Pittsburgh Civic Arena and drew 8553 fans, when some kids went on a tear, breaking store windows and damaging nine city buses. Twenty-five were arrested and 22 treated at city hospitals. Damage to the hall itself, though, was "next to nothing," according to the hall's general manager. And Paul Martha, the arena's vice-president, noted, "We had five altercations inside the arena, and that is not unusual for a crowd of 9000."

Pittsburgh's Public Safety Director John Norton decided to go on the attack, however, insisting in a front-page story in the *Pittsburgh Press*: "There is no question in my mind that the disturbance was drug and alcohol-related. Groups like this are ruinous to the morals of our young people. The lyrics in the songs are provocative and pornographic."

Pittsburgh Mayor Richard Caliguiri was equally vexed: "I will no longer stand for this hooliganism. . . . We may have to cut out some of these shows that come into Pittsburgh if our young people don't know how to maintain some sanity when they come out of them." Ominously, he added, "We'll sure find out if the city has the authority to ban concerts."

Russell, naturally enough, fired back. He released an angry statement to the press in Pittsburgh, which began: "My groups are internationally esteemed for the high moral content in the music they make. The songs performed this past Saturday night encouraged the audience, among other things, to stay in school, to vote, to stay away from drugs, to value monogamy, and to believe in each individual's ability to achieve whatever he wants through plain old hard work.

These rappers are nothing less than heroes to an audience which otherwise sorely lacks them."

Warming to his topic, the senatorial Mr. Simmons now shifted into a higher gear. "And, on the eve of the Fourth of July, what else do Pittsburgh's young blacks, yearning to be free, have to celebrate? Rigorous public education? Decent public housing? Extensive, safe, cheap public transportation or health care? Public safety in the black community? Equal opportunity under the law? Jobs? The maddening answer is none of the above. What young black Pittsburgh has is rap, and now the city wants to take even that away. It's an outrage."

Happily enough, Pittsburgh City Controller Tom Flaherty agreed. "The issue isn't the concert," he told the *Pittsburgh Courier*, a black weekly newspaper. "The issue is that we're sitting on a time bomb. Situations such as Saturday's are a telling indicator of the city's lack of concern for the black community."

Public Safety Director Norton was unpersuaded. A few days down the road, according to a story in the *Pittsburgh Press*, Norton hatched a plan of dazzling weirdness: he would have the city hire early Sixties teen idol Bobby Vee, whom Norton praised as "a community resource," to read in advance the lyrics of the rock acts due to play Pittsburgh, in an attempt to predict which groups might cause trouble. Designed to protect the youth of Pittsburgh from wild rockers and rappers, this plan somehow failed to foresee that the solution might be worse than the problem: After Bobby Vee had cleaned up, who would protect Pittsburgh's young people from the singer who had so wantonly inflicted "The Night Has A Thousand Eyes" upon an unsuspecting world so many years before?

In fact, the natural tendency of the Raising Hell Tour to draw thousands of young black kids together in cities where they were usually confined to the ghetto often inflamed the local media. Less than a week after the Pittsburgh show, the newspapers in Cincinnati had a field day over, well, over nothing much at all. The controversy started out red-hot. "YOUTH FIGHT DOWNTOWN AFTER CONCERT" blared the front page of the *Cincinnati Enquirer* on July 7. The *Cincinnati Post* chimed in with "CURFEW TALK GROWS LOUDER AFTER CONCERT" over a story that claimed "a crowd of 8000 roamed downtown after the show."

But the next day the *Post* was running a much smaller and quieter story under the headline "Chabot Likely to Drop Demand for Curfew," which had a local city councilman reporting that the sum of the rampage was three arrests for disorderly conduct and one broken window. Finally, Chabot's boss waded into the fray. "It is not a crime to be young and black and downtown after dark," counseled Mayor Charles Luken. "We have to be careful not to blow things out of proportion because of race and age."

And sure enough, once the newspapers took race and age out of the story, the proportions *did* change. The story got smaller and smaller and was pushed deeper and deeper into the paper, until on July 10, a one-paragraph story on page 2C of the *Post* quietly announced, "Chabot Won't Push for Youth Curfew." This was not at all as sexy as the front-page story that pictured 8000 black youths roaming around downtown after dark, and undoubtedly was read by far fewer people.

The tour pulled into Madison Square Garden in hometown New York on July 19. Once again there was some trouble after the show, and once again the media blew it all out of proportion. The show was a sell-out, with 20,000 tickets sold. The extent of the trouble inside the arena, according to MSG spokesman Bobby Goldwater, was 81 chairs damaged by kids standing on them to get a better look at the onstage action. The next day's *Daily News*, however, claimed that "groups of teenagers rampaged through surrounding streets harassing and robbing pedestrians" and that 38 arrests had been made. In a slightly more sober report, The *New York Times* claimed, "18 Are Arrested After Rap Concert."

It wasn't until August 9, in a story reported in *Billboard* by Nelson George, that reality began to intrude. "Despite local news reports linking several midtown Manhattan arrests to a recent rap show at Madison Square Garden, most of the incidents may have had nothing to do with the concert, according to police and show promoters," wrote George. "News coverage linked the gig to robberies as far away as 27 blocks from the midtown venue, and included incidents reported hours after the show's 10:50pm end."

This kind of distortion and bias naturally upset the crew. "All of us rappers get a raw deal by the newspapers, man," Run said. "Just because it's black people, they think we ain't got nothing to do except bust somebody's head open. That's bull. Rap music and rappers are about making people—especially young people—feel good about themselves. Because most older people and almost all white people don't understand it, they got to down it. I just wish they'd chill out and stop hassling us."

None of this was to deny that the tour had a persistent problem. As Jeff Sharp noted, "At several shows on this tour, there have been about one hundred knuckleheads who show up outside the hall to cause trouble, which doesn't mean that we should stop doing these shows and deprive the majority of the 20,000 who had a good time."

Those "knuckleheads" were career criminals who came to

"get paid." They weren't fans of the music and they hadn't bought tickets. They simply waited around outside the hall until the show was over, and then attacked Run's fans knowing that they'd probably get away with their little robberies because these bad kids looked like the people they robbed, which made it easy for them afterward to blend into the crowd. To that extent, New York's most sensationalistic daily newspaper, the *Post*, was also the most accurate in its coverage of the Garden show. Their headline? "WOLFPACK PREYS ON GARDEN CROWDS"—which correctly identifies the crew's fans as the *victims* in this situation, not its perpetrators.

Run understood it all very clearly. "We can't go to heaven and perform; we out here with the bad people," he said. "We got to put as much positive message behind it as we can, but we can't stop the devils."

Indeed, some writers accused Run-DMC themselves of devilishness. Don Thomas of *Big Red*, a Brooklyn-based black newsweekly, was offended by some of the cursing onstage. "Cursing is not bad to me," Run responded. "Every little kid curses, although he may not curse in front of his mother. The curses are like punctuation marks in our raps. They are the commas, periods, and question marks."

It was harder to deal with public criticism from their old friend Kurtis Blow. When *Newsday* asked Kurt about contemporary rap lyrics, Kurt said, "Those lyrics are bad. 'Time to get ill' means go crazy, time to stomp somebody's face off. What Run-DMC is doing is perpetrating, acting like they're tough gangster kids when they're not. And the kids see Run acting that way, so they try to be gangsters." Months later, Kurt confessed that he'd attacked the crew out of "envy in my heart." Reversing himself in an interview with *New*

York magazine, he said, "I think their music is great, and I'm proud of them." The funniest and most revealing comment, though, is Kurt solemnly swearing, "If they were in trouble, I'd be right there for them with a Uzi."

All of these minor incidents—in Cincinnati, Pittsburgh, and New York—were put into proper perspective by the gang riot at Long Beach, which was, as noted, the one date on the tour where there was trouble *during* the show, *inside* the arena. Despite the tour's security precautions, there was no way of predicting the trouble that developed in Los Angeles. Indeed, it was a problem that appeared to be beyond the control of the Los Angeles Police Department. "Ten years ago nobody cared about gangs because they were essentially killing each other," said Captain Bob Martin of the LAPD's Detective Support Division. "But now that they've moved into robbing and stealing drugs for profit, outsiders are involved." And, he told the *L.A. Sentinel*, "They certainly can't come to us when they've been ripped off, so their only form of getting back at each other is murder."

And that only describes the situation in L.A.'s crack-selling black and Hispanic communities. The white punk and heavy-metal scene is just as wild, with every rock club in Orange County having been shut down due to violence over the past few years, according to an article in *Spin*, which concluded, "Kids come to L.A. to find trouble, much in the way they went to Berkeley and other California campuses to riot in the late Sixties."

In retrospect, Run-DMC had been blindsided. They'd played the Los Angeles Sports Arena with the Raising Hell tour on May 30 without incident, and they'd been a huge smash at the Los Angeles Street Scene Festival in 1985 on a bill with Stevie Wonder, Richard Pryor, and Joan Rivers. For that matter, only the night before Long Beach, the tour had played to 15,000 fans at a sell-out at the Oakland Coliseum, which had gone off, according to promoter Bill Graham, with "not one single problem."

Long Beach, then, was something else. Not only was it home to the Insane Crips, an especially demented chapter of one of the L.A.'s largest gangs, the arena itself had a history of violence that stretched back 15 years. According to the *Long Beach Press-Telegram*, there'd been 46 arrested at a Jethro Tull show in 1970, 21 arrested after a 90-minute battle with police at a Ten Years After show in 1971, 31 arrested on drug charges at a Led Zeppelin show in 1972, a 17-year-old security guard murdered at a rock concert in 1977, a stolen car rammed through the arena's back entrance by a fan of the Marshall Tucker Band in 1979, a young kid seriously injured when he fell from a balcony onto his head during a Deep Purple show in 1985, and a riot the very next day by one thousand fans of Iron Maiden and Twisted Sister, who went berserk after learning, following a nightlong vigil, that the site of the box office had been abruptly changed. Finally, less than three months before the Raising Hell Tour, a drug-addled kid at an Ozzy Osbourne show had broken his neck and died after slipping on the arena's floor, while 50 others were arrested on minor charges over the course of the Oz's three-night stand.

The only really outstanding question about the Long Beach show is why it took the Long Beach police so long to respond to the promoters' calls for help. Darryll Brooks began calling at 7:35pm, when the fighting first started, and called every 15 minutes thereafter until 10:30. The police would turn around and phone the managers of the arena, who kept insisting, "We have everything under control. We don't need you yet."

This was at a show that had already ground to a halt by 9pm due to gang-fighting, which would continue to rage until the police finally arrived after eleven o' clock! Darryll suggests that the management's footdragging probably betrayed their embarassment—to call in the police would be to admit that they couldn't safely operate their own arena.

In any case, the riot instantly became international news. Smelling blood, Tipper Gore, of the Parents Music Resource Center (an anti-rock lobbying group) attacked rap—and heavy metal. "Angry, disillusioned, unloved kids unite behind heavy metal or rap music, and the music says it's okay to beat people up," she informed *USA Today*. Russell quickly responded. "Instead of attacking rap, Mrs. Gore ought to spend some time investigating the sources of the anger and disillusionment she sees in America's youth," he said. "I'm sure she'll find that rock'n'roll is not part of the problem, but part of the solution." Run likewise had some advice for the PMRC. "They're out to get us, but I'm not hurt," he said. "I have three albums—take 'em home and listen to them and call me in the morning." Jennifer Norwood, one of Mrs. Gore's sisters in the PMRC, did just that, and had to admit, "None of us has had a chance to see Run-DMC live in concert. On the *Raising Hell* album, there's nothing in the lyrics that is really explicit or would incite kids to violence."

Still, the shock waves emanating from Long Beach would be a long time susiding, and the people who ran the arenas on the rest of the tour's dates were suddenly very nervous. At first the reaction was merely comical. "Run-DMC Concert Crowds Calm, West Palm Beach Police Report," announced the *Miami Herald*. "Rap Group's Greenville Appearance is

'Routine,'" reported *The State*, out of Columbia, South Carolina. These headlines over stories reporting that there was no news to report were very reminiscent of the satirical guest column Rick Rubin wrote for the *Village Voice* on August 19. Addressing the fact that "only 18 arrests were made by an anxious, media-inflamed police force [at the Madison Square Show], the headline of the *New York Post* the next day might have read: 'NO ONE KILLED AT RAP SHOW; AUTHORITIES PUZZLED.'"

But they weren't laughing in Providence, Rhode Island. The license for the show set for August 28 in the Civic Center there was revoked by the city's licensing board. "Prudence dictates that if a dog bit someone yesterday, you don't let him loose tomorrow," said Police Inspector Michael Brugnoli.

In truth, the rappers and the city shared some history. The Fresh Fest had played the Civic Center the summer before and drawn a sell-out crowd of "13,000 black and white teenagers," according to *Boston Rock* reporter John Nordell. "Demand was high," he continued, "and the police used questionable amounts of force, including a wild policewoman on a horse, to clear out the several thousand ticket seekers turned away at the door." Run-DMC returned the following December with the Rock & Rule Tour to play the Living Room nightclub in a show described by the *Providence Journal* as "trouble-free."

Journal music critic Mike Boehm thought that local authorities were making the wrong move this time. "It isn't always easy to play in the big leagues of arena entertainment. Providing security for an act like Run-DMC is like having to face Nolan Ryan's fastball. But if you're a pro, you don't call off the game. You do what's necessary to stay in it."

Unfortunately, the problem in Providence didn't really

have much to do with professionalism. The unequal application of Inspector Brugnoli's Mad Dog Rule tips us to the real story. It seems that heavy metalists Judas Priest had been allowed to play the Civic Center on June 5, just one week after a teenager was stabbed to death at their show in Tacoma, Washington. The Providence show, according to local police, was "a real horror show: lots of alcohol, lots of drugs." Maybe the Priest show was allowed to go on in Providence while Raising Hell was barred because, as Kathy Haight of the Knight-Ridder newspaper chain noted, the Priest concert death only "produced four paragraphs on the national wire services."

Haight turned to Rubin's *Voice* column for an explanation of the different ways these similar situations were handled: "The problems that people have with rap concerts have to do with society's own troubles with black youth, not with a lyric from a Run-DMC record. . . . Music is not the problem. Racism is."

And so the Raising Hell Tour limped through its last few U.S. dates, reaching Washington, D.C.'s Capitol Centre on August 31. "The Raising Hell Tour has been portrayed as some sort of pop music plague," the *Washington Post* noted. "But as Saturday's performance made clear, the show is just another package tour. . . . Although things got a bit raw in places, the general tone was overwhelmingly and undeniably positive." Which serves as a fair description of 63 out of the tour's 64 shows.

Indeed, for those music lovers undistracted by the reports of violence, the Raising Hell Tour was one of the great events of the season. David Hinckley summed it all up in a *Daily News* story that ran on September 10—"From a good concert summer, one image gets stronger looking back: Run-DMC taking on the Garden like a small club and mesmerizing 20,000 fans as if they were clutched in Run's fist. Rap's got many stars, but none demonstrates the power of this music, or rock'n'roll, better than Run-DMC.

"To say rap inspires crime is dangerously distorted," Hinckley continued. "A teenager in California killed his grandmother last month because she interrupted his Bible reading. So do you blame the Bible? Of course not. You say, 'This kid had problems that happened to surface right then.'

"And there you go."

NINE

Tougher Than Leather

When Run-DMC and the Raising Hell Tour left America for England and a tidy little two-date postscript at London's Hammersmith Odeon on September 13 and 14, they undoubtedly thought they were leaving controversy behind them. In fact, once they got to London, things were cool, but the Brits definitely had an overheated idea of the tour's history.

"After the right royal visit of Prince, the year's most highly anticipated tour [is] Raising Hell, the package that [has] rampaged across America to volatile audiences of warring ghetto gangs," wrote *Melody Maker*. As it turned out, the Brits *loved* the tour, there was no violence, and the show likely could have sold out the elegant 3500-seat Odeon for a week or more.

"Everyone was there, all mixed up," reported the *New Musical Express*'s Dele Fadele. "Downtown scenemakers, tough-stance hardhats, celebrities, media hawks. . . . Beastie

Boys paced the stage like b-boys from Saigon, all handslaps and leers . . . LL came across like Chuck Berry, Louis Armstrong, Miles Davis and James Baldwin all sharing a toke on Stravinsky's toenails. . . . "

Echoes's Evie Arup provided a distinctly feminine take on the show. "LL's performance was nothing short of impressive, especially when he tore off his shirt and grabbed his dick, an act which left some of the females clustered around the front in various stages of arousal. The Ladies Lurve Cool J, make no mistake. . . . "

The *London Times*'s David Sinclair now picks up the tale. "By the time Run and his partner DMC had both reached the stage, it was pointless to clap. The audience had come well prepared with whistles and hooters; the screeching clamour reminded me of old footage of the Beatles, when the sound of the band is frequently drowned by a cacophony of screams. . . . They consistently generated the sort of primitive excitement that used to be the norm at early rock concerts."

The crew themselves was thrilled with the reception—and even warmed up slightly to the native cuisine. "People always say the food's bad in England," noted a thoughtful Run. "But now they got McDonald's, so I eat french fries."

Back in New York Run-DMC began to gear up for two major anti-crack events. As kids who'd grown up in the city and rockers who'd seen as much as they cared to of the seamy side of the fast life, the crew was not about to jump on any bandwagons. They got involved because they knew this plague was destroying *their* community, Hollis, Queens. Crack was the drug now being sold on the corner.

"Some musicians want to get involved, but we *need* to 'cause it's our kids who are doing this," said Run. "It's more addictive than heroin. You take a puff of it and it's over. Your ambition to play basketball is gone. Your ambition to think is gone. You don't want to go to school. Next thing you know, you've taken your sister's VCR and her earrings to buy some more of the stuff. It only cost $10 a time, but you have to keep having more." DMC recalled walking around in the neighborhood and being approached by an older woman desperate for the drug. "She was a nurse about 40 years old, and she thought I might be a crack salesman," D mused. The crew had grown up a lot since their days as high school dabblers. Now none of them had anything to do with drugs.

Run-DMC was already planning to headline a huge LiveAid-styled anti-crack rally at Yankee Stadium at the end of October, when New York City's Mayor Koch asked them to join an event he had planned for the morning of October 7. Called "Don't Crack—Not Even Once,' it was sponsored by the *New York Post*, organized by the Board of Education, and held in Madison Square Garden's Felt Forum. Former New York Knicks great Earl Monroe was there, as were three of the New York Rangers and boxer Renaldo Snipes. Matilda Cuomo, wife of New York Governor Mario Cuomo, addressed the 4000 junior-high and high-school kids present, and then Mayor Koch hit the stage.

The mayor told the kids that they had a bright future without drugs, and that from among their ranks would come the future leaders of the city—"In this crowd today there is an Ed Koch, and someday you will take my place." He then led the crowd in an anti-drug pledge and swore them in as members of his Student Anti-Drug Squad.

But, as the Associated Press noted, "There was no doubt about who had top billing. Whenever Run-DMC was mentioned, the decibel level soared. The response when they took the stage was euphoric—and deafening." The crew made a very brief speech about it being hard enough to make it in this world straight and how doing drugs made it much harder. They offered themselves as an example, and let the kids know that there was no way that Run-DMC could do what they had to do if they used drugs.

Then Run had a couple of questions for the crowd.

"Y'all gonna do drugs?" he asked.

"No!!!" screamed 4000 teenagers.

"Y'all gonna go to school?"

"Yes!!" they all screamed back .

"Good!" he said, and kicked the crew into a special anti-drug version of "It's Like That." The next day they flew to Los Angeles to prepare for KDAY's Day of Peace.

The second anti-drug rally took place on October 31 at Madison Square Garden. It was an impressive event, but as originally conceived it was *earth-shaking.* Apparently, at just about the same time that Run-DMC were getting concerned about crack, so was concert promoter Bill Graham. Graham, of course, had not only produced the Live Aid show in Philadelphia, he'd produced a giant six-city stadium tour on behalf of Amnesty International—an organization that fights for the rights of political prisoners—which featured Sting and the Police, U2, Peter Gabriel, Jackson Browne, Lou Reed, Bryan Adams, and Joan Baez.

A recent chance visit to New York, where he'd lived between the ages of 11 and 21, convinced Graham that now was the time to do something on a large scale that addressed a specifically American problem—crack. "I went to a newsstand in the Village, where I lived for years, and they were selling these large glass pipes," he recalled. "I bought one for $17, and the irony of it all was that on the side of the pipe was an 'I Love New York' logo. Somehow that sticker drove home to me the outrage of people making a buck off someone's casket, and how complacent we've become."

Once Graham and Run-DMC joined forces in an event called Crackdown, to be held at Yankee Stadium in the Bronx, it looked like the sky was the limit. An organizational meeting held at the Carnegie Deli in New York attracted not only Mayor Koch but dozens of political, music business, and religious bigwigs. The idea was to get as much cooperation as possible from everyone who wielded power in the city, so that the event itself would go off without a hitch.

The unforeseeable hitch was that *none* of the superstars who'd lent their talents to "We Are the World" and "Live Aid" and "Farm Aid" and the Amnesty International Tour could be convinced to sign up for this event. Graham, who wanted the money raised by Crackdown to fund a permanent citywide drug awareness and education agency, and who worked like a dog trying to line up artists, was baffled. The only explanations he could come up with were that the issue was too exclusively New York-identified, and that the superstars were "aided out."

In the end, Crackdown had to be scaled down considerably. Eventually there were two shows held back-to-back at Madison Square Garden. On October 31 the bill featured Run-DMC, the Allman Brothers Band, Crosby, Stills & Nash, Santana, Ruben Blades, and the great Nigerian drummer Olatunji. The next night was an all-Latin artists show with Tito Puente, Santana, Ruben Blades, Willie Colon, Eddie Palmieri and Bobby Rodriguez.

It remained a good cause, of course, and Run-DMC was proud to be a part of Crackdown. Unfortunately, the crowd at their show—comprised largely of aging hippies—had some trouble accepting Run-DMC, the one act on the bill who came from the street. These hippies showed up for a look at Sixties "survivors" Crosby, Stills & Nash and the Allman Brothers Band, each of which included notorious drug abusers.

David Crosby was a cocaine addict who had been released only the previous August 8 from Huntsville State Prison in Texas after nine months in jail on drugs and weapons charges. Greg Allman was a former heroin addict and cocaine abuser who testified against his drug-supplying road manager in exchange for immunity in January of 1975. Having saved Greg's life after the rocker's near-fatal overdose in 1974, this road manager was swiftly sentenced to 75 years in prison.

Critic Wayne Robins, covering the show for *Newsday*, really let the hippies have it. "There was no sense of the unity that gives uplift to the best benefit concerts," he wrote. "The battle against ignorance has a long way to go. You would have thought that Run-DMC, who have done more to fight crack than all the other acts put together, would at least be treated with respect for those efforts. And you'd think that 'Walk This Way' would've made the predominantly white audience realize that there was at least some musical common ground to be explored.

"No way. Evidently, there are still hordes of white people who become apoplectic at the sight of black people displaying aggressiveness anywhere but the boxing ring, basketball court, or football field. Run-DMC drew obscene shouts from people who might have grooved on the rappers verbal heavy metal if they'd only listened."

Elvis Mitchell, in an amusing review for *USA Today*, noted: "In the biggest irony in any event espousing peace, love, and brotherhood, the chart-topping rappers Run-DMC were loudly booed. The pair seemed oblivious to the crowd's reaction—maybe because their onstage bodyguards looked capable of beating up the entire house."

Run-DMC were not oblivious. They were disgusted, and they left the Garden immediately after their set, before chummy group photos of all the acts on the bill could be shot.

It was during that same jam-packed month of October 1986 that the crew made three important network television appearances. On October 2, the entire half-hour of comedian David Brenner's "Nightlife" was devoted to Run-DMC. The crew performed "Walk This Way" and "My Adidas," but the highlight occurred when Brenner brought out a sneaker he'd worn when he was 14. "Look at these holes!" he said with warm nostalgia for his lost youth. "These sneakers ran the streets of West Philadelphia."

Run grabbed the antique shoe from Brenner, shot a quick glance at it, said, "These are weak!" and tossed it on the floor. Brenner got his own back a few minutes later when he asked to examine Run's shoe and then sailed the laceless Adidas off into space. At the end of the show, the style war over, the two combatants hugged. Afterward, Run sent Brenner a pair of fresh *new* kicks.

On October 18 the crew performed on "Saturday Night Live," which was hosted that night by Spike Lee, the great young writer/actor/director behind the independent film "She's Gotta Have It." Spike and the crew were cast together in a skit that made fun of Run-DMC's violent image. In the guise of Mars Blackmon, the b-boy hero of "She's Gotta Have It," Spike stood onstage explaining to the studio audience and all the folks watching on TV that no matter what they may have read in the papers, his homeboys Run-DMC were *not* violent, that their terrible reputation was the result of a big media conspiracy, and so on. Meanwhile, "backstage" we see the crew beating the stuffing out of "SNL" producer Lorne Michaels, who'd made the critical mistake of accidentally scuffing Jay's sneaker. Run-DMC leave Michaels crumbled up on the floor, step over his body, and take the stage to perform "Walk This Way."

Two days later Run-DMC were in Los Angeles to appear on "The Late Show Starring Joan Rivers." The crew busted out "Walk This Way," sat down beside their host, and introduced themselves with a rhyme from "Darryl & Joe" —

Run: Well, have you heard, I'm the first and I'm
         number one
         Not the best, not the worst 'cause my name is
         Run
DMC: And I'm second 'cause I reckon that you want to
         see an emcee like D inside the place to be
Both: And have you heard that he is third and his name
         is Jay
Run: I'm Run, the ace
DMC: D, the deuce
Both: And J's the trey!

The studio audience was still applauding this snappy little display of skills when the irrepressible Ms. Rivers—always eager to get in on the act—rocked a little rhyme of her own: "I'm Mama Joan and I'm here to say, I got my own show and I'm here to stay!" At the end of the interview, Joan slinked up on top of her desk, chantoozie-style, slipped on a homburg hat, and had the guys read a rhyme off the teleprompter with her . . . something to do with her show being "the best in the U.S.A." and promising to be right back after the next commercial. Later, the guys were constrained to sit there while 80-year-old John Houseman discoursed on the subject of Great Acting. . . .

Just before Christmas Run-DMC flew with their families to Japan for a series of dates in Kobe, Toyko, and Nagoya, December 18–22. The shows were held in 2000 to 3000-seat halls and the crowds were enthusiastic. But what really stunned the crew were the Japanese b-boys. These young fanatics had *all* the right gear: Kangols or velours on top, sheepskin coats, and Adidas on their feet. Most amazingly, they had the *attitude* down, and knew how to chill hard in a b-boy stance. If they ever develop Japanese rappers, it may be all over.

❖ ❖ ❖

Run-DMC shot the entire 95-minute feature film entitled "Tougher Than Leather" in the 26 days ending on December 9. The movie's plot is simple. Runny Ray, Run-DMC's roadie and lifelong friend, is found shot to death backstage at one of their shows alongside a known drug dealer. Police investigators arrive at the conclusion that the two dead men killed each other in a disagreement over a deal. Run-DMC, who knew Ray too well to believe that he had anything to do with drugs, try to convince the police that Ray's been framed. When the police decide instead that the case is closed, Run-DMC are forced to solve the mystery of Ray's murder to clear his good name.

"It's not a true story," Run said, "but it's going to be real." In other words, though the story told in the movie is completely fictional, "Tougher Than Leather" is true to the tougher-than-leather image of Run-DMC. This stands in contrast to "Krush Groove," which was based on several true stories, but which was essentially false in its portrayal of Run-DMC because of Hollywood's fear that making the picture too tough would mean bad box office. This time, Jay said, "Hollywood is exactly what it *won't* be. It'll be *Hollis*-wood, a movie from Hollis in Queens. We hire the director and we can fire him when we want."

In this case, the director was Rick Rubin, who'd created a new company with Russell called Def Films to make "Tougher Than Leather." Most of the money came from Run-DMC themselves —and from Rick and Russ—which meant that the creative control would stay in their hands. The script was written by Rick and an old college pal named Ric Menello from a story by Lyor Cohen and B. Adler. When there were beefs, it was all in the family. Holliswood.

Although he'd studied film and video at NYU and directed the music video for the Beastie Boys' "She's On It," Rick had never before directed a feature-length film. His lack of experience, however, did not slow him down. "I was a little scared about making this movie, but there isn't anybody who knows more than I do," he said. "I was on the set of 'Krush Groove' watching Michael Schultz direct a scene between Run and the guy playing his brother Russell, and everything he was saying was *wrong*. It really made me mad. I read the script. I understood how to get those emotions. It's the same thing when you're making a record. So I stepped in front of him, and I said, '*No!* That's *not* how it goes! *This* is how it goes!' And I directed the scene. Then Schultz said, 'Excuse me, Rick. Come with me for a minute.'

"Now this was taking place on the corner of a theater stage. He put his arm around me, walked me all the way across the theater really far before he said anything—like you take someone really far away because something bad's gonna happen. So he said, 'Rick, I appreciate your enthusiasm. But there can only be one director and I'm the director, and don't ever do that.' And I said, 'I'm really sorry, but it was really making me mad because once you put it on film, that's the way it's gonna be, and it's gonna be wrong.'

"So we walked back. And the guys who were doing the scene said, 'What should we do?' Schultz told them, 'Do what Rick said.' And they did, and it was good.'"

In retrospect, a humbler Rick admitted that making movies is not quite the snap he'd imagined it to be. "It's very hard work," he said. "It's many more hours and much more tense than making records. There's much more at stake all the time. You have a staff of thirty people always waiting for the next thing to do. It's very tough."

Even while "Tougher Than Leather" was still in production, there was some concern about the amount of violence in it. Comparisons to "Rambo" were surfacing. Rick countered that the movie will appear to be more violent than it actually is. "There isn't that much killing in this movie," he said. "It's just that it is going to *seem* violent because there is a lot of tension and drama and confrontations."

"It's gonna be like a good John Wayne flick," said DMC. "The violence is there, but you don't mind if the good guys are doing it."

"You're happy we're kicking their butts," added Run. "At the end we're all heroes."

Just like in real life.

Bad As Ever, and Clever

Run-DMC's story is one of almost continuous success. Not only have they made it big, they've done it their way, with no compromise and no sell-out. "Three outlaws from the music trade. We don't rob, but our job is to get paid," rhymed D, which is a fair summation of their whole approach. Of course, making it to the top, and *staying* there are two different accomplishments, and the reason Run-DMC has been number one for so long is because they not only know where they're going, they know who they are, and where they've been.

Every interviewer they talk to these days wants to know how success has changed Run-DMC. They're big stars now. Why don't they move to Hollywood? Run knows why. "That's corny and fake, man. If Michael Jackson is happy out there, more power to him. Onstage I'm being an actor a lot of the time. I know when to change, and when I get off the stage, all the ego that you see *drops*. And then I become Joseph Simmons.

"When I'm back in Hollis, I'm not out there wearing chains and trying to act tough," he continues. "I'm a family man. I just need two dollars in my pocket and a basketball game. I don't want anything. I'm so happy. I look at my daughter sleeping. I kiss her while she's asleep. I go into the basement and work on some music. Next day I get up early, wash my car, see some of my friends, go into the studio. My wife does the dishes, I take out the garbage. It's a real *organized* life. I just bank the money I make, and I'll live in Hollis till I die, probably."

DMC, who still lives at home with his folks, is also happy. In fact, as John Leland captured him in an article for *Spin*, D can be "beatifically content." "Today I ain't got nothin' to worry about," he told Leland. "I washed my car. I gave my friend some money, he gonna pay me back tonight."

More importantly, as Jay has pointed out, the crew is happy *together*. "We are lifelong friends. We are closer than anyone can imagine," he said. "Run-DMC is more than a band. It's more like a bond. We have everything in common. If I didn't have a wife and baby, and Run didn't have a wife and baby, we'd probably all be living in the same house."

All this togetherness, however, doesn't mean that being Run-DMC isn't hard work. It is. "The way I see it, it's no pain, no gain," says Run. Speaking of the "Tougher Than Leather" soundtrack, which he and the crew were then working on, he continued, "If things don't fall into place, I'll just have to make 80 records and then pick ten for this album. I might make *90!* But I'm not going out like a roach. And going out like a roach is giving up. You can spray Raid on my back and I'm gonna carry it with me wherever I got to go, do what I gotta do. Cause it's like this to me—I gotta have it right or I'm gonna be real mad that I don't have it right. That's how we number one now. I get so into what I'm doing 'cause I don't want to lose real *real* bad. So when I don't win, I won't be here."

In the meanwhile, Run-DMC take their day-to-day responsibilities to their fans very seriously. "Kids look up to us and we give them something good to look up to," Run said. "I'm a great guy. I went to school. I don't do drugs. So it's no problem for me to be a role model. We want you to look up to us. Please do. I'll give you the right step. I ain't gonna send you the wrong way, baby-pop."

All of which leaves us with the question of Run-DMC's commitment to rap, the musical fad that was supposed to have gone the way of the Twist and the hula hoop years ago, and which only seems to grow stronger and stronger every season—eleven years after Russell Simmons first saw Eddie Cheba in a Harlem nightclub, and ten years after 12-year-old Joey Simmons invented a big bragging emcee named DJ Run, Darryl McDaniels dreamed up a terror named Easy D, and Jason Mizell put aside his bass and started scratching records in the park as Jazzy Jase.

Run-DMC are still very young men, but they've already devoted over half their lives to the music they love. They did it for fun before they got paid, they're still doing it for fun now that they're getting paid and, when they look to the future, they see themselves rapping away at the top of their lungs as old men.

"People are always asking us, 'If rap dies out, what do think you'll be doing?' DMC says. "We tell them, 'If singing dies, what's Aretha Franklin going to do?' They ask, 'Are you ever going to start singing love songs?' We say, 'No! We'll rap till our hair turns gray.'"

Or as Run says, "I'm sure rapping's gonna last forever." In other words, their *own* words, the Kings from Queens fully intend to continue "causing hard times for sucker emcees 'cause they don't make no rhymes like these."

Period.

R.I.P. JMJ, 1965–2002

On Wednesday night, October 30, 2002 I was helping my son with some schoolwork when the phone rang at about 10 o'clock. It was a reporter from the *New York Times* wondering if I knew who had shot Jam Master Jay. As my heart leapt into my throat, I told him I had no idea what he was talking about and that he must be mistaken. Then I turned on the tv and saw that it was true. There on the street outside Jay's recording studio in Jamaica, Queens, were DMC, Chuck D, Lyor Cohen, and hundreds of local citizens trying to console each other as Jay's body was removed from the building. Jam Master Jay had been shot in the head, execution-style, and murdered. A week later, after Jay's funeral, Run and DMC announced the retirement of the group.

It was the only thing to do. Run-DMC was a trio and Jam Master Jay was always their anchor. In performance he was to Run-DMC what the drummer Charlie Watts has been to the Rolling Stones: a superb timekeeper and an engine of funk. In hiphop terms, Jay was not especially flashy, but he was a master of the cut, a real-time editor who kept the show moving and the energy high. If Run-DMC was one of the great live acts in hiphop's history, Jason deserves a large part of the credit. And he was just as influential in the studio, where his production ideas had a crucial influence on Run-DMC's recordings for years and years. Finally, there could never be a substitute for Jay as Run-DMC's fashion guru. "Jam Master Jay dressed so well that the fellas hated to go shopping with him," DMC joked at Jay's funeral. No, better to close up shop. "I can't get out onstage with a new deejay," said Run. "I don't know any other way but with the three original members."

In the immediate aftermath of Jay's death, tabloid pundits were quick to suggest that this horrible crime was the latest grim example of the wages of gangsta rap. Anyone with even a passing familiarity with Run-DMC knows that this is absurd. Run-DMC weren't gangsta rappers, and not only wasn't Jay himself a rapper of any kind, he was a notably peaceful person. Indeed, as the introductory chapter of this book indicates, Jay was explicitly *anti*-gangsta from very early in his career.

Jam Master Jay was a musician and mentor of musicians and what he was doing on the last night of his life was entirely typical — he was producing an album by a new recording act. Jay had begun exploring a variety of new creative ventures as soon as Run-DMC's blazing mid-Eighties hot streak starting cooling off. He formed Walker Wear, a line of hiphop apparel, several years before Russell Simmons founded Phat Farm in 1992. He discovered and produced Onyx – a kind of younger generation punk-rap version of Run-DMC – for his own JMJ label. And in the late nineties Jay was among the very earliest mentors of a young rapper from Jamaica, Queens named 50 Cent.

But if Jay wasn't a gangsta, he also wasn't a saint. He was somebody who needed to keep his ear to the street, if only because that's where the new talent is. And, sure enough, the word on the street is that Jay was shot by someone he knew, someone who'd decided that Jay owed him money. If that's true, then Jay's murder was quite senseless. It had nothing to do with "gangsta rap," and everything to do with the all-American tendency to settle disputes with guns — and the epidemic tendency of young African-American men, in particular, to kill each other with guns.

At the funeral, the MC formerly known as Run, now better known as the Reverend Run, struggled to make sense of Jay's senseless death. "You ask, why murder?" he said. "Well, Jason was a dramatic deejay. He couldn't just leave without drama, so why *not* murder?"

For all the cosmic acceptance implicit in those sentiments, I don't share them. Jay was indeed a drama king, but he had no hand in the design of his final exit. He did not kill himself, he was murdered. He was 37, with a wife, three children, a mother, a sister, a brother, hundreds of friends, and millions of fans all around the world. Until his murderer is found, his death will be an open wound. When and if the murderer is found, the mystery of *why* Jay was murdered will remain.

But there is one point on which Run and I definitely agree: there was exactly one Jam Master Jay and he is irreplaceable.

— Bill Adler
May 2003

Index